A Derby View

A Derby View

The Best of Anton Rippon

Anton Rippon

First published in Great Britain in 2010 by
WHARNCLIFFE LOCAL HISTORY
An imprint of
Pen & Sword Books Ltd
47 Church Street
Barnsley
South Yorkshire
S70 2AS

Copyright © Anton Rippon 2010

ISBN 978 1 84563 137 6

A CIP catalogue record for this book is available from the British Library

Typeset by Acredula

Printed and bound in England
By CPI

Pen & Sword Books Ltd incorporates the Imprints of Pen & Sword Aviation, Pen & Sword Family History, Pen & Sword Maritime, Pen & Sword Military, Wharncliffe Local History, Pen & Sword Select, Pen & Sword Military Classics, Leo Cooper, Remember When, Seaforth Publishing and Frontline Publishing

For a complete list of Pen & Sword titles please contact
PEN & SWORD BOOKS LIMITED
47 Church Street, Barnsley, South Yorkshire, S70 2AS, England
E-mail: enquiries@pen-and-sword.co.uk

Website: www.pen-and-sword.co.uk

Contents

Introduction

One of my favourite cartoons is from that wonderful 'Peanuts' series by the late Charles M. Schulz. It shows Charlie Brown's pet beagle, Snoopy, receiving a letter from a publisher to whom he has submitted a novel.

The letter reads: 'Please find enclosed two rejection slips. One is for the book you recently sent us. The other is for the next book you write.'

Rejection: it's the writer's worst fear. Well, after writer's block, which is when you can't think of anything to write about in the first place.

And when this afflicts a weekly columnist, it can be a terror. George Bernard Shaw tried it for a few years on *The Spectator* before giving up because, he said, he felt like a man standing under a windmill. Just when he'd dodged one sail, the next sail was bearing down on him . . . and the next and the next.

There's a joke among the fraternity: Why don't writers stare out of the window in the mornings? Answer: because they'd have nothing to do in the afternoons.

As my old friend and occasional co-author, Andy Ward, is always quick to me: 'When you're a writer, you're only ever one letter away from being a waiter.'

So, in the eight years that I have been writing a weekly column for the *Derby Telegraph*, I've always had my feet on the ground. And when two old friends, Subrata Dasgupta, who logs on from his home in Louisiana, and Ken Walker, who lives a lot nearer, in south Derbyshire, independently suggested that it would be a good idea to put a collection of the columns into book form, I wasn't so sure.

But, over the years, enough readers have been kind enough to write in to say that they were enjoying the weekly offerings. So I began to think that it might be appreciated after all.

There are no particular themes. How the columns tumbled out depended on whatever happened that week, or whatever bee was in my bonnet at the time. The same bee sometimes makes a reappearance. Occasionally local politicians wandered into my sights. Sometimes it was just the daft side of life that set me off. Often it was no more than a chat with regulars down the pub; or me pleading with family members to come up with an idea. Almost without exception, the columns appear here as they originally appeared in the newspaper.

Whatever, altogether I hope the writings give a feel for life in my hometown, now, and in the past, with an occasional nod as to what it might be like in the future.

I thank former *Derby Telegraph* editor Mike Norton for first giving me the opportunity all those years ago. And I am hugely grateful to his successor, Steve Hall, for developing the idea into a feature of his newspaper.

Anton Rippon

Derby, 2010

LITTLE GREEN MEN IN ALVASTON PARK

Imagine it. You've sped across several thousand light years, from another planet in a far distant galaxy. You're homing in on Earth and you're wondering where to land. You flick the pages of your inter-galactic equivalent of *Foder's Travel Guide* and you're spoiled for choice – the Grand Canyon, Victoria Falls, Great Barrier Reef, the Pyramids. Maybe even Aztec ruins in Mexico. The world really is at your fingertips.

So why would you choose Alvaston Park? It's a question that's been bugging me ever since the Ministry of Defence released details of a spinning cylindrical object with red, blue and green lights around its middle, that was sighted a few years ago, apparently touching down behind a building in the DE24 postcode. Dovedale, I could understand. Matlock Bath, even. But Alvaston Park?

To be fair, September 1995 wasn't the first time that a UFO had been spotted hovering over that particular Derby suburb. According to the records of Burton Abbey, back in October 1253, a bloke called Nicholas of Findern was wandering through Alvaston when he saw two smaller stars fighting a battle against a larger star. Sparks began to fly and he was joined by a large crowd 'stupefied by fear and ignorant of what it might portend'. Eventually, they all ran off and now we'll never know.

So call me an old cynic, but you have to think that perhaps Nicholas had been at the mead, that night in Alvaston all those years ago. And what was he doing there anyway? It's a fair walk from Findern, even today.

Then again, there may be something about Alvaston that attracts people from Findern. And little green men from the other side of the universe, too. Although if they wait 750 years between visits, then whatever it is, it can't be all that compelling.

Actually, Alvaston isn't just the site of Derby's first recorded UFO sighting. It is also the spot where the second recorded Derby earthquake took place. That was reported in the *Derby Mercury* in October 1750. So maybe there is something mysterious going on in Alvaston. It probably won't be long before someone mentions leylines. And local ghostbuster, Richard Felix, has organized a walk.

But where else in Derby would space tourists find it worth their while to visit? If the cast of that old Smash commercial does confront us, we must be prepared. So, on your behalf, I've given it some thought. And, to be honest, I'm struggling.

I'd certainly think that Darley Park would be a better bet than Alvaston. And you might be able to persuade them that the Quad was an alien craft that had landed in the Market Place by mistake. But we need Marketing Derby here. Anyone that can put a spin on Green Lane (one of the city's 'hidden gems') could surely dream up a case for Derby to be high on a Martian's itinerary. Personally, I'd just take him to the Rowditch Inn for a pint.

In the meantime, we also have to consider what we'd do if a 3ft bloke with a television aerial sticking out of his head wandered up and demanded: 'Take me to your leader.' I suppose we'd have to get him down to the Council House to see if Hilary Jones was in residence. Although, having taken the trouble to watch the occasional council meeting on line, I'm not sure that he'd get the warmest of welcomes. The leader does seem to give short shrift to anyone who isn't a Lib Dem.

But at least she might be able to make our space visitor answer that nagging question: What is so special about Alvaston Park?

DERBY'S WOES – IT'S JUST COMMON SENSE

You can put all manner of things to rights while leaning on the four-ale bar. The war on terror? Bring back our troops from Afghanistan

14-2-'11

Dear Joan

I thought you might enjoy reading Anton Rippon's latest book. I had him sign it.

Don't be shocked when you see my ugly mug gracing the photo collection

I hope this finds you well

Love
Stan

and instead spend money and manpower on shoring up our own borders. Crime? If someone is sentenced to 10 years, make sure that they serve 10 years. Derby County's Championship struggle? Just nip out and buy another Dave Mackay. No problem is insoluble if you have a pint of best bitter in your hand.

Indeed, by its very definition, playing the game of 'If I were in charge' is always rewarding. You aren't actually in charge. Therefore you don't have to produce the actions that would bring to fruit the solutions you've scribbled on the back of a beer mat.

None the less, there are times when I wish that I were in charge of Derby City Council. I'm sure you all do (not all wish that I were in charge, obviously; just that you were). We all believe that we've got the answers, most of them just a matter of common sense, really. We just can't understand why, these days, common sense is such an apparently rare commodity within Derby's corridors of power.

Hospital and university parking, public toilets, bus lanes, the Hippodrome – you name it and a good dollop of common sense would probably solve it, albeit one person's solution can quickly become another's problem. You can't please all of the people all of the time.

But you can please most of them. In fact, when it comes to the Hippodrome, you could probably please all of them. And if I were in charge, I'd do it tomorrow.

For two years, Derby City Council has apparently sat on a suggestion from Derby Civic Society that a good chunk of the area marketed as The Lanes – broadly speaking, Babington Lane, Green Lane and Gower Street – should become a conservation area.

You'd think that the council would be sympathetic. After all, its city centre management website boasts: 'Situated in the heart of Derby, The Lanes feature a variety of interesting buildings, which illustrate architectural trends from the mid-19th century through to the 1960s . . . making it a thriving and pleasant place to visit.'

The reality is that the area is far from thriving and pleasant; in fact, it is quite run-down. But it is home to several listed buildings and if conservation area status were granted, then the dear old Hippodrome would become eligible for an English Heritage grant. And what a great starting point that would be towards rejuvenating the area.

The council already markets The Lanes as 'Derby's hidden gems'. Once the theatre was restored to its former glory, it would become the main jewel in that crown. It doesn't take a great leap of imagination to see families pouring out of a wonderful old theatre and into bars, restaurants and small independent shops in a revitalized part of Derby.

Why the council hasn't acted on the society's suggestion is not clear, although it may have something to do with persistent rumours that it is hoping to tempt a supermarket chain to take over the old Debenhams site. If that were to happen, then a road would be needed from the inner ring road extension to the supermarket car park. And you can't go driving one of those through a conservation area.

If the area was so designated and the Hippodrome saved, then everything else would almost certainly follow. The present hollow marketing slogan would actually begin to mean something. Personally, I'd forget about Tesco.

But then, I'm not in charge. I'm just leaning on the bar.

EAST MIDLANDS POLICE FORCE? NO THANKS

A hospital waiting room can be a soul-destroying place. With its oppressive heat and terminal boredom, you could lose the will to live just by sitting there.

Hopes can soon be dashed. You've been given an exact time to attend, so you think, well, if they've worked it out that precisely . . . Then you realize that 49 other people have also been told to turn up on the dot at 10.20 am.

After two hours of mind-numbing daytime television (whatever ailment you came in with, you're now also suffering from a stiff neck because the TV set is ceiling-mounted), you consider pointing out that you also have a life and would like to get on with it, please.

But complaining isn't really an option because nurses wielding hypodermic needles have always been high on your list of people not to annoy.

You've read all available copies of last year's Sunday supplements, and you've set all the NHS posters to music (The old 'Coughs and sneezes spread diseases, so trap the germs in your handkerchief' works beautifully to the tune of *Deutschland uber Alles*).

Of course, you daren't go to the toilet because, inevitably, that is when your name will be called and you'll go straight to the back of the ever-lengthening queue.

So I am happy to report that none of this was the case when I had to visit the Pulvertaft hand unit at the Derbyshire Royal Infirmary a few days ago. A cyst on a tendon in my left hand is causing problems. I can accept the pain as payment for not having to help with heavy shopping or gardening, but the condition is seriously inhibiting my ability to carry two pints, unspilled, from bar to table, an essential part of my Friday lunchtime. A sympathetic GP referred me to the world-renowned Pulvertaft unit. They apparently once treated Prince William; if it's good enough for a future king of England, then it's obviously good enough for a commoner like me.

The staff are wonderful and, in less than half an hour, I was examined by an unfailingly courteous consultant who decided that an operation was necessary.

But, waiting my turn, I picked up a leaflet in which the Derbyshire Police Authority canvassed opinions on Government plans (seemingly about to be aborted, as it turns out) to create a single East Midlands police force.

The leaflet asked whether an East Midlands force would save money and be better at tackling serious crime. Well, sharing intelligence would certainly be a good idea, but you'd like to think that this was already being done; a quick e-mail here and there would probably sort it out.

More likely, local concerns would suffer: Derbyshire would enjoy only one-fifth of the members of an authority that would also cover Nottinghamshire, Lincolnshire, Leicestershire and Northamptonshire.

And although the Government said the cost of setting set up the new force would be £80 million (how can re-badging a few thousand policemen's helmets be so expensive?), it would give only £28 million towards the merger. So what services would suffer in order to find the shortfall?

But the best reason to have voted against the plan was simply that the Government believed it to be a good thing. Whenever a politician assures us of anything, the exact opposite usually happens. If they announced that it was going to get dark this evening, I wouldn't wager 10p on having to switch the lights on. And how thoroughly had the leaflet been circulated? I picked mine up by chance. Perhaps a few people waiting for operations to their hands decide the future of local policing.

LAYABOUTS? MOVE THEM ON – AGAIN AND AGAIN

Derby Market Place: a disparate collection of obviously less than upright citizens had spread themselves on the steps of the war memorial. One young man, in particular, wasn't entirely comfortable. He wriggled a bit, then abandoned his attempt on the world record for the fewest bites it takes to demolish a 12ins-pizza, and investigated.

Would you believe it? Someone had been inconsiderate enough to place a poppy wreath on the memorial. He tugged in irritation at this tribute to the Falklands fallen, pulled it from beneath him, and resumed his bid for a place in the Pizza Chomping Hall of Fame.

The young man captured perfectly an issue that has been engaging many Derbeians in recent weeks, although in the interests of fair play, I must also report that the man next to him, who was laying waste to an ice-cream, looked old enough to have been rescued from a Dunkirk beach. So paying scant respect to our war memorial isn't just an age thing.

Nor is anti-social behaviour restricted to upsetting old soldiers. A few yards away, a pack of feral youths, each of whom seemed to have sidestepped the process of natural selection, were lolling by the water feature, spitting aimlessly on the ground. And, incidentally, is there anyone that can ever walk past that water feature without thinking that 10 quids' worth of quick-growing ivy would make it look a lot less like a sewer outlet?

Meanwhile, across the Market Place, a notice above the graffiti adorning the tourist information centre, announced: 'You Are Being Videoed.' To what effect I cannot imagine. Perhaps graffiti vandals can now buy DVDs of themselves at work.

On the subject of raising money, while at the same time attempting to make the centre of Derby a safer and pleasanter place, another sign cautioned that skateboarders and cyclists could be fined £500.

I can't, however, recall anyone ever being up before the beak for such an offence, much less being made to 'fork out a monkey' as they say at the races.

Yet it could be so different. Years ago, I had the great pleasure to visit San Antonio, Texas. The river walk there is a major attraction. Yet it wasn't always so.

An American colleague told me that, at one time, it was a place where few decent people dared venture. To cure the problem, the city did more than put up a few notices; it employed security guards to constantly harass and move on that small but significant minority whose only object in life seems to be to spoil things for the majority.

While Derby's Market Place yobs ignore notices, they would presumably respond to being harassed by someone who looks a bit more threatening than the mayor.

I've long felt that a relatively small amount of money spent on some heavy-looking security staff would be very well spent. If you kept moving people on, they'd soon get fed up.

And while we're on the subject of the Market Place, isn't it about time that Derby's tourist information centre was moved from that dreadful building next to the 1970s Assembly Rooms, and into the wonderful 1840s Guildhall that graces the Market Place itself? Imagine a visitor, new to Derby, asking for directions to the tourism office and eventually finding themselves confronted by what has all the appearance of being stuck under a motorway flyover. It would take you all your time not to turn tail and flee back to the station and the first train home.

Note: Derby City Council subsequently placed studs around the war memorial. The situation is better. But not much.

Human Story Behind a Newspaper Cutting

Maurice Searcey was sorting through his late mother's possession when he came across it – a yellowing newspaper cutting from the *Derby Daily Telegraph*, dating from March 1916. It was the sort of news that had become depressingly familiar 90-odd years ago: Private Thomas Brown, aged 39, of the 10th Battalion, Sherwood Foresters, had been killed 'in France'.

In fact, in the fog of war, the report wasn't entirely accurate. Private Brown had actually died in Flanders, killed in action during the British counter-attack on the Ypres–Comines Canal. His body was never found and he is one of 54,896 Commonwealth soldiers who died without graves and who are commemorated on the Menin Gate.

More to the point, as we near Remembrance Sunday, he was Maurice's grandfather. Last week, Maurice showed me the cutting as we enjoyed a beer at Mickleover Golf Club. And, as we supped, he told me the human story behind those facts so starkly reported at the time.

Before he joined up, Thomas Brown worked for Derby Corporation and lived at 38 Mundy Street, in Derby's old West End. He left behind a widow, Sarah, and seven children, none of them old enough to work.

When he was himself growing up, Maurice would sit on his grandmother's knee while she told him of the days of struggle that followed the death of her husband in a foreign field.

To make ends meet, Sarah obtained a job at a yeast mill in Leiper Street, working from 6 am to 6 pm. An unusually kind employer (for those days, at least) allowed her to pop back home at 8.30 am, to ensure that her children were all up, washed and ready for school.

Remarkably, that seems to have been the only help that Sarah Brown ever received. In the years after the end of that war, which was supposed to end all wars, anyone collecting money for the British Legion poppy appeal knew to give 38 Mundy Street a wide berth. Otherwise they would have received a fierce broadside from a woman left to fend for herself and her family, despite her husband's sacrifice.

As the leaves tumble from the trees, this can be a melancholy time for anyone who has lost relatives in war, be it in the greater slaughter of 1914–18, in Afghanistan today, or on any battlefield in between.

A couple of years ago, as autumn turned to winter, we were in Flanders visiting the cemeteries of the Great War. There are so many war cemeteries in Flanders that you can't visit them all. So, on a cold, grey November day, we drove past the one at Lijssenthoek, a few miles west of Ypres. I wish we'd stopped: I later discovered that my great-uncle, Alexander Craig, is buried there. Like Thomas Brown, he also lost his life fighting with the 10th Sherwood Foresters, in September 1915, aged 25.

Remarkably, Alexander died only a few miles from where he first saw the light of day. My great-grandfather was a travelling salesman and in 1876 the family was living in Bruges where Alexander was born. The Craigs ended up in Derby, and it was from here that he answered the call to the Colours.

We'll think about him this Sunday, and also remember Uncle Eric, lost in the North Sea in 1941, when a U-boat torpedoed his merchant ship. We'll also remember cousin Sid Rippon, laid to rest in a war cemetery in Milan. Sid was fighting with the New Zealanders when he was captured in the Western Desert and then had the misfortune to contract appendicitis in his PoW camp. War touches most families over time.

THOSE VETERANS MUST FEEL LET DOWN

What a difference a day makes. First there was the dignified 84-year-old who recalled being marched into a prison camp on his 17th birthday, and the 70-somethings who were only children when they escaped aboard the last ships to leave before the bombs fell. Later, there were the world-owes-me-a-living layabouts of modern life, the sort that must make the others wonder if their sacrifices were ultimately worthwhile. From dignity to despair – it takes only a few uneasy steps in today's Britain.

Scene One was a military club in Piccadilly, where a reunion of those who'd been in the Second World War's Malaya campaign was under way. The old soldier had joined the volunteer forces on the outbreak of hostilities. He was still a teenager when the Japanese put him to work on the Thai–Burma railway. Sixty-seven years on, he smiles a lot. But he still suffers nightmares.

Most of the others had been small children in 1942, the offspring of planters and civil servants working for the British Empire on a part of the map that was still solidly red. Their stories were remarkably similar. After the Japanese invasion, their fathers had spent the next three and a half years – if they survived – in the dreadful Changi prison, or on the Death Railway. The children had fled with their mothers as Singapore capitulated.

To be honest, I felt something of a fraud at this gathering of folk dedicated to keeping the families of the British Malayan volunteer forces in touch with one another. I had no shared experiences. I was there simply to keep alive the memory of my own relative, cousin Fred, who'd served as a volunteer before spending the rest of the war in Changi. So it was enough to stand and listen – and in some awe, too.

Scene Two was Derby city centre, the following day. There was a time when everybody in the middle of Derby looked busy, as if they were going to, or coming from, somewhere. But now there were many who appeared to be just hanging about. Some were scruffy; others well dressed. Some look like foreigners; others were obviously locals. Some were in groups; others alone. They all had one thing in common, though: they didn't appear to be going anywhere, or coming from anywhere. At least certainly not anywhere that might provide them with gainful employment.

If I'd been a brave man, I'd have approached at least one or two, and asked a very simple question: 'Excuse me, I'm dying to know – who pays your wages?' But I think that I already knew the answer: indirectly, you and me, dear reader. I'd be very surprised if the relatively young people who can apparently afford to loll about all day in Derby, often drinking strong lager, aren't on some kind of benefit. I don't care whether they arrived yesterday, hanging under a container lorry from Calais, or whether they can trace their origins right back to the primordial soup that once sloshed around this particular bit of Merry England. I'm not bothered whether they are from Timbuktu, or whether neither they, nor their ancestors, have ever set foot outside the ring road or its prehistoric equivalent. I'd just stop the benefits of anyone whose sole idea of a career path is learning how to fill out a claims form.

We used to say that life was all about the haves and have-nots. Today, it's more about the givers and the takers. Those Malayan veterans and their children gave a lot. Sometimes they must feel terribly let down.

A Walk to Derby in Mellow Mists

Nice time of year for a walk, early November. Funny sort of time, too: still Keats's season of mist and mellow fruitfulness – but only just. The nights are drawing in fast. Next Wednesday is Armistice Day.

Then, before you know it, the Last Post will sound for the year itself. *Tempus* does indeed *fugit*. It doesn't seem five minutes since people were letting off fireworks to celebrate the dawn of a new millennium. Now we're almost at the end of its first decade.

Come to think of it, people are always letting off fireworks. Diwali, Bonfire Night, New Year's Eve, Chinese New Year, every Tom, Dick and Harriett's birthday – this year, someone in the next street even celebrated the Fourth of July; the excuses for disrupting the neighbourhood with industrial strength gunpowder seem never-ending. There, that's that particular grumble out of the way. Now back to the matter in hand.

I needed a haircut (it happens every autumn). It was still 15 minutes before nine o'clock and I had three options: wait three-quarters of an hour until the free bus pass kicked in; pay the bus fare;

or walk the two and a half miles from Chain Lane to Cheapside.

I wanted to get on, but the second option wasn't really an option at all. You don't get much for free these days (not unless you're a career benefit claimant), so forking out £1.90 for the sake of 45 minutes didn't appeal.

In any case, I have decided to take more walks. And as it was one of those wonderful late autumn mornings – cloudless blue sky, slight nip in the air – I put my best foot forward, humming a selection of George Formby standards as I went forth. And yes, before you ask, quite a few people think I'm barmy.

Anyway, I'd been plodding along for about 10 minutes when a man came up and asked if I had a pair of jump leads. Strange question to put to a pedestrian, especially one giving full vent to 'When I'm Cleaning Windows', but he was desperate. His car battery was flat, the vehicle stuck in a bus lane and, unluckily for him, I was the only one around. I suggested Kingsway fire station, then hurried on my way before he could ask for a push.

It wasn't a particularly illuminating experience (I'm still not sure what jump leads do) but, overall, you'd be surprised at the variety of things you can learn while walking into town.

For instance, I can tell you where to find abandoned Sainsbury's shopping trolleys, what time Uttoxeter Road cemetery closes (I'm going to explore that soon), and that the big house opposite Bemrose School is all sad and boarded up. Fifty years ago, when it was in its pomp, I used to stare at that house from a chemistry lab, wondering who could possibly afford to live there. In those days, appearing attentive while daydreaming was a particular skill of mine.

Back in the present, it was a grand day for a good walk. Nice and still. Not too warm, not too cool. Add in the leaves in their full rustic majesty, the occasional dew-jewelled spider's web, and you can begin to see why John Keats was moved to compose that famous ode.

Of course, it was an autumnal evening walk in early 19th-century

Winchester that inspired him. What he would have come up with had he stumbled upon Derby's inner ring road extension on a busy Wednesday morning in 2009, I can't imagine.

It makes you think, though. I wonder if that man ever got his car started.

OINK'S FENCE IS NOW MY WEIGHT LOSS GAUGE

It all started when we discovered the cost of a day return train fare from Derby to Skegness, and then I couldn't squeeze through the gap in the fence to see Oink, the water buffalo. I'll explain: way back in the summer, yours truly and those two pals from Gerard Street days, John Burns and Colin Shaw, fancied a day out at Skeggy. But then we learned that the train fare was something like £38 (if you pick the right day, you can get to London for half that).

True, there was a cheaper fare, but you had to leave Derby so late, and return so early, that to catch a glimpse of the North Sea would have involved a sprint from Skegness station and then a dash to catch the train home.

And that was supposing that three gentlemen, well into their 60s, could have managed all that running in the first place. Especially someone like me, who has, shall we say, the fuller figure.

So we cast around for alternatives – Felix Buses' attractively priced day trip to the same resort was fully booked – before settling for a stroll around Darley Abbey. Maybe not as much fun as a day at the seaside, but thoroughly pleasant for all that.

And this is where Oink, Derby's famous grazing water buffalo, originally a gift to the local vicar from an Indian village, came in. A keen angler, John is a regular visitor to these parts. So he knew about a small gap between the gatepost and the fence that surrounds Oink's field.

I'll now probably get him arrested for trespassing, but John said that he often slips there to get a closer view of the 15-year-old gentle giant. And, to be fair, Oink always seems pleased to see him, despite the fact that, in recent times, the poor beast has had his fair share of unwelcome visitors.

But when I tried to get through the gap to join John, I couldn't. In fact, I almost became stuck. The headline, 'Fire brigade called to *Derby Telegraph* columnist wedged in fence', flashed through my mind.

Anyway, after I'd managed to extricate myself backwards, I suggested that Colin had a go. Just to see if it was me, or whether John has some deformity, not immediately visible to the naked eye, which enables him to squeeze through small gaps. Colin was having none of it, and I can't say that I blamed him.

So, we left Oink staring balefully at us from the bottom of his field, and, while I can't pretend that this was a Damascene moment in my life, it did make me realize that, once and for all, I should try to lose some weight.

After all, notwithstanding health issues (not to mention the embarrassment of becoming stuck in fences) there are the clothing practicalities. My wardrobe contains a line of perfectly good trousers, the waist sizes of which go up in two-inch increments.

It was hard work at first, but once you realize that you don't really need two high-nutrition breakfast bars with your evening pot of tea, it can be achieved. So last week I couldn't wait to climb the scales during my six-monthly MoT at our local surgery. Normally I try to distract the nurse by asking about her holidays, so when this time I volunteered to be weighed, she knew that something was afoot.

And, yes, a whole 9lbs had been shed. The following day, I visited Oink again. I'd decided to use the gap in his fence as a gauge to my progress. Alas, there appears to be much work still to do.

'WHAT ARE THEY DOING TO DERBY?'

Here's a leap – memory lane and back again, via a salacious newspaper headline. It had been the usual jolly evening in the Rowditch Inn: lots of chatter, a roaring fire on a chill February night. Just like pubs used to be. But it was time for my companion to leave. He'd driven down from Tyneside the day before, primarily on business, but also to call into the city – it was only a town when he left all those years ago – where he was born. Now it was catch-up time.

Last orders were being called when, with some considerable reluctance, we left the cosy scene and stepped out into the freezing night air.

There was a brief pause while we conducted a final bit of reminiscing about those long-gone days at Bemrose School, just a few yards up the road. Then I turned up my coat collar and made for the bus stop, while he went to find his car.

A few moments later, he was on his way with a cheery last wave, heading into the city centre and his bed for the night.

A few minutes later, my phone rang. It was my pal.

'That was quick,' I said. 'Forgotten something?'

'No,' he said, 'but I've just had a shock. 'What are they doing to Derby? They seem to be tearing the soul out of the old neighbourhood. It's all deserted streets, apparently undergoing some kind of open-heart surgery.'

By his description, I think he must have found himself down by the work going on to extend the inner ring road. It would certainly have been in stark contrast to the convivial evening we'd just enjoyed.

'The soul went out of it years ago,' I told him. 'It's just that it's been finally ripped apart. They call it Connecting Derby.'

I can understand how shocking it would have been to someone who hadn't set foot in Derby for 40 years or more. You never expect to find things exactly as you left them. But it's still a jolt when you realize that your old world has all but disappeared.

The next morning, on my way into town aboard one of Trent Barton's finest, I went through the edge of the same area. Yes, it must have surprised my pal: all those little streets that he remembered, now razed to the ground, a yawning expanse of mud and rubble where once families sat around their fireplaces on cold winter nights.

Anyway, I was leaning over the shoulder of the man in front, trying to read his newspaper (he'd not paid for it either; it was one of those free ones) when the headline, 'Lecturer who offered degrees for spanking', caught my eye.

Unfortunately, the man alighted before I could read further. But it made me wonder. Was the lecturer offering degrees in return for this service? Or was he actually running a course in that ignoble art?

My money was on the former, although the latter wasn't beyond the bounds of possibility. At various UK universities, you've recently been able to take courses in stand-up comedy, stained-glass window studies, bed selling and body piercing. So why not in the administration of corporal punishment for recreational purposes?

Now, I'm as broadminded as the next bloke. But, the more I thought about it, the more I realized that I didn't want to know. Sometimes, ignorance really is bliss.

Which makes me wonder if my old pal now wishes that he'd stayed away and settled for remembering Derby the way it used to be. As I said, it's a bit of leap. I believe they call it lateral thinking.

DID TERRORISTS DO THIS? NO, DERBY CITY COUNCIL

Stan Guy wanted a walk around the old neighbourhood. It had been half a century since he'd last trodden the streets between his former home in Rowditch Avenue and Becket School in Gerard Street, which we both attended until 1956.

'What do you think?' he asked. 'We could just wander about the old area and maybe have a pub lunch halfway through.'

It sounded like a plan, but I warned him: 'It's changed a bit since your day. We'll probably need body armour. Last month someone fired a shotgun at a front door in Parliament Street.'

'Blimey, it has changed,' said Stan. 'We just used to ring the doorbell and run off.'

'Come to think of it,' I said. 'you could get some material for your next book.'

When he left Derby Technical College in 1963, Stan went to work for MI5 (although no one told him at the time), then became a high-flying international banker before embarking on a third career as an author of best-selling crime fiction set in Tokyo, where he now lives.

He dismissed the idea of his hero being transferred from Tokyo Central to St Mary's Wharf: 'I can't see Inspector Nishii investigating crimes in Stockbrook Street.'

'Fair enough,' I said, although I still thought it had potential.

I arranged a tour of the highlights and we met at the Heritage Hotel in Macklin Street, so first I had to show him the pile of rubble that was once Duckworth Square.

'Who did this?' asked Stan. 'Al-Qaeda?'

'No,' I said, 'Derby City Council.'

Stan was particularly pleased to see the stage of the Hippodrome, where he'd watched many a panto, although puzzled as to why he could now view it from the other side of Crompton Street.

I explained: 'This out-of-town property developer was trying to repair the roof and it was a spectacular case of "Sorry, it came off in my hand".'

'I wouldn't like to see anything he was actually trying to knock down,' said Stan, gazing mournfully at a bit more of his demolished past.

We pressed on to Gerard Street, where Stan was disappointed to find that Becket School had disappeared.

'Still,' he said, 'at least there's a nice bit of green here now, with lots of trees.'

'Not for long,' I told him. 'The inner ring road is coming right through here.'

Abbey Street didn't lift his spirits and I wasn't sure how to break the news that Rykneld School, where he'd spent four years, had also long since fallen victim of the wrecking ball.

But there was a corner shop here, a pub there, that he remembered and, as we settled down in the Olde Spa Inn, Stan pronounced our stroll down memory lane well worth the drive up from London.

The previous summer we'd met for the first time in 50 years and he made me eat raw fish and seaweed in a Japanese restaurant just off Oxford Street. I returned the compliment, although this time the fish was battered and came with chips and peas.

We wandered back towards his hotel and, after I'd reminded him where the Black Prince cinema used to be, he said: 'I'll walk with you to the bus station.'

'Er, no you won't,' I said. 'They knocked it down several years ago. But we are getting a new one. It's just been delayed while they teach the drivers how to reverse into it. I know. Don't ask.'

Later, when I opened the copy of Stan's book, *Touchline Samurai*, that I'd asked him to sign, he'd written: 'To a friendship renewed.'

He could have added: 'To a city demolished.'

QUESTIONS, TELEVISED COUNCIL MEETINGS, VICARS

I've never been one for completing questionnaires – especially when the compiler feels it necessary to promise that they'll take my views into consideration. Why else would they want to know them? It's mostly that they're trying to kid everybody that someone is taking notice before whatever scheme they've already decided upon is introduced.

The last one I completed related to facilities at Derby railway station. As a regular user, I thought it worth a shot. Needless to say, none of my well-formed recommendations ever came to pass; and I can't believe that a lot of other frequent travellers didn't tick the same boxes that I did.

Then a questionnaire from Derby City Council dropped on the doormat. It was from the grandly titled Overview and Scrutiny Officer, and concerned the proposed reorganization of the eight Derbyshire primary healthcare trusts.

Apparently the council's Social Care and Health Overview Scrutiny Commission – I'm not making any of this up, by the way – was carrying out a review of proposals contained in a consultation document issued on behalf of the Government by the Trent Strategic Health Authority. Phew!

From what I understand, it boiled down to whether we should have one primary care trust for the whole of Derbyshire. Or whether Derby should have its very own.

But while the Overview and Scrutiny Officer wanted me to let him know which option I favoured – and if I returned the form early enough, he'd enter me into a prize draw to win £100 – nowhere did he tell me the benefits of either option.

Now, if I'm honest, I don't think that I'd be prepared to wade through a Strategic Health Authority consultation document, even if the Overview and Scrutiny Officer had enclosed one, but a few bullet points on the matter would have helped.

True, I can call with queries. But I don't believe that the Overview and Scrutiny Officer is expecting an avalanche of calls asking: 'Have you got a spare hour to explain the differing benefits of one primary care trust or two?'

There is a health authority website. But many of the people likely to be most worried about health issues don't even own a computer. I've returned the questionnaire – you never know your luck, and

£100 always comes in handy – but I'll have to put my tick in the 'Don't Know' box.

Meanwhile, eager to support any kind of initiative that supports local democracy, I went on the internet to view recordings of Derby City Council meetings. Gatherings of the full council can be seen on its website; and if watching paint dry is too exciting for you, then you can always try the proceedings of the planning committee. All in glorious colour.

The downside is that everyone sounds as if they're doing an impression of Norman Collier, the 1970s comedian who did a routine where his microphone kept cutting out. Whether our elected representatives are going to follow this up with Collier's famous chicken walk, or the one where he pretends to blow on a bag of hot chips, I don't know.

But it would enliven debate and crank up the viewing figures. We could even fix up the mayor with a cloth cap and a concert secretary's bell.

Finally, a friend confesses to a feeling of guilt whenever she is approached by a police officer. Even though she knows that she has done no wrong.

I sympathize. I have the same problem with vicars. As soon as I'm in the company of someone wearing their collar back-to-front, I begin to feel guilty, about what I have no idea. And don't even mention nuns.

WHEN CLOUGHIE RUINED DURBAN'S EGG ROUND

You can never chat to Reg Harrison, one of two survivors of Derby County's 1946 FA Cup-winning team, without feeling a whole lot better for the encounter. With his beaming smile and infectious chuckle, Reg is one of nature's true gentlemen. It's also most unlikely that you'll be able to talk to him without at least half a dozen of the

Rams' more mature fans coming up to shake his hand.

Most recently, we met in the tinned fruit aisle in Sainsbury's, having both been despatched by a respective spouses with instructions to replenish supplies depleted over the festive period.

There was a time when it was not at all unusual to see professional footballers shopping in town, even on the morning of a match. Of course, those were the days when football was, quite emphatically, a working-class game.

Players and fans often travelled together to matches, on the same Corporation bus. Derby-born players like Reg, Tommy Powell, Bert Mozley, Ray Young and Jack Parry were more than happy to mix freely with the fans. Indeed, any local footballer really was part of the community.

In fact, when Reg's playing days were over, he became a painter and decorator, and then worked for Derby Borough Council's parks department, coaching young boys in the art of trapping, dribbling and shooting for goal.

I recall emerging from the Regent billiards saloon in Babington Lane one Saturday morning, just in time to witness Rams player Albert Mays – an excellent snooker player who hailed from Alvaston – grab a supporter by the throat; the man had apparently made an unflattering remark about the fiery Albert, who was, a few hours later, due to run out at the Baseball Ground.

Also in the early 1950s, Derby defender Geoff Barrowcliffe would play against the likes of Manchester United or Tottenham Hotspur, and then be first out of the bath and running towards Friargate station where he would catch the teatime train back home to Ilkeston in order that he might help his mum with some last-minute shopping on Ilkeston market.

Terry Webster, Derby's goalkeeper in the days when they won the Third Division North, delivered meat for a butcher in the afternoons and Alan Durban recalls how the arrival of Brian Clough proved wholly inconvenient to his own little sideline of re-selling eggs that he'd bought from ex-player, Brian Daykin. The egg round was carried out in the afternoon because players trained for a couple of hours in the morning and then had the rest of the day off. The likes of Albert Mays spent that free time in the snooker hall, while some, like Alan Durban, used it to supplement their income with a little job. When Clough introduced afternoon training sessions, that cosy world disappeared.

And the entire Rams team that was crowned kings of English football in 1972 could always be found each Saturday evening, celebrating with the regulars of an Allestree pub. What happy, uncomplicated days they were.

I suggested to Reg that, eventually, the Derby County Former Professional Players' Association (of which I am overwhelmingly proud to be an honorary member) will struggle to enlist members. Today's have-boots-will-travel players come in from foreign lands, play a season, then continue on their mercenary way. Even the British ones are often here only for a month's loan.

You can't blame them for that. But it's unlikely that, in 30 years' time, any Rams supporter will be enjoying a chat with Arturo Lupoli by the trifle sponges in the Westfield Centre. Or find Mart Poom cycling up to his front door with the Sunday joint in the basket of a butcher's bike.

CAN YOU IMAGINE CHICK MUSSON IN A LEOTARD?

Funny how, as soon as you meet them, some people want to tell you their life story. Impressive, how much they can pack into a 15-minute bus journey.

He'd boarded in Osnabruck Square on his way to the Royal Derby, called back to discuss an eye test that had followed a diagnosis for diabetes. Before we'd turned into Macklin Street, I knew his name, his age (same as me, it turned out), that he lived near Ripley, and that he'd been a coal miner all his working life.

By the time we'd reached the Rowditch, I was fully aware that he didn't think much of Arthur Scargill. And that, although he had suffered a serious injury in a Derbyshire pit accident (for which he'd never received any compensation) until the day he died his father had spent long hours on his allotment to put food on the family table.

My new friend couldn't understand why he'd got diabetes. He'd never smoked and he'd always kept himself fit. He was particularly keen for me to know that he'd been a good footballer. But his liking for the ale had ensured that his career never took off. He could, he said, sympathize with George Best.

That's another funny thing: football skill relates inversely to age. According to the rheumy eye of memory, the older a man gets, the better player he was when he was young. The former miner was certainly happy to bracket himself with one of the greatest footballers who ever lived, although the only similarity seemed to be that they both liked a drink.

Between there and the hospital, he contented himself with addressing the state of the game, especially how it was being ruined by fancy-dan foreign footballers who got paid far too much. Then, with a firm handshake and an 'All the best, squire,' he was gone. And I was left wishing that the journey had lasted a bit longer, because his machine-gun delivery of a well-rehearsed party piece had left no daylight for debate. Not that I would have disputed his argument over today's footballers.

I'd have just said that when, in *The Good Companions*, J. B. Priestley described the importance of a football club to a community – 'To say that these men paid their shilling to watch 22 hirelings kick a ball is merely to say that *Hamlet* is so much paper and ink' – he was talking about the cloth cap and muffler brigade of a different age.

Funnily enough, that very evening our phone rang and on the

other end was an England footballer who did indeed epitomize those days. And he wanted to talk about fancy-dan foreign players.

Bert Mozley left Derby for Canada over 50 years ago, although he's never bothered to acquire an accent and still sounds as if he's never strayed far from his native Chester Green.

'I can't believe it,' spluttered Bert. 'I've just watched Arsenal and Atletico Madrid on the telly. It's August, yet one of the players is wearing gloves – and a leotard. Can you imagine Chick Musson wearing a leotard?'

Of course I couldn't imagine one of the Rams' toughest-ever players dressing up like a ballerina. Nor apparently spend several hundred quid on having his hair permed, which was something else that was distressing Bert about this fancy-dan foreign footballer.

Of course, Bert's Derby County included many players who came from Derbyshire itself. They travelled to matches on the same Derby Corporation buses as the fans. Shopped at Derby Co-op, like everyone else. Some of them had even worked down Derbyshire pits.

I think that Bert would get on well with the ex-miner from Ripley.

Lew Is Still a Good Old Sport

I've said it before: if ever I feel the urge to exercise coming on, I lie down until it passes. That's not to belittle those who love to run.

It's just that I've never been keen on the idea of jogging. Traffic fumes, the possibility of getting something called shin splints, or being run over, or twisting an ankle on a dodgy pavement, not to mention horror stories about internal organs moving around – it sounds a positively dangerous pursuit.

But pounding the streets of Derby has apparently never harmed a wonderful character who has just celebrated his 96th birthday. In fact, Lew Patrick, a stalwart of Derby and County Athletic Club – now Derby AC – when it boasted some of Britain's finest athletes, was still running every day until he was 83. So what do I know?

When I was a lad, Lew was a familiar figure on his training runs in our neighbourhood. However, unlike some veteran athletes – they know who they are – Lew is no self-publicist. His own trumpet remains defiantly unblown. But I think that Derby AC should strike a medal for him. Not that he's short of a few after a sporting career that spanned 70 years.

He was 14 when he went to work at the Carriage and Wagon, alongside Jack Winfield, an English international three-miler, who one day invited him to try out for Derby and County AC at its headquarters at the Wagon and Horses on Ashbourne Road. Lew was soon representing the Midland Counties AAA against Combined Universities in a cross-country event.

He was also a good footballer, turning out for Second Division Bury's reserve team: 'They offered me professional terms, but I was earning more at the railway works. And it would have cost me my amateur status in athletics. I wouldn't have been allowed to compete.'

In these days of Usain Bolt's huge earning power, that's hard to imagine. But instead of big bucks, 'shamateurism' was rife, according to Lew: 'Athletes would sell or pawn their trophies – gold watches, canteens of cutlery, silver cups. Work was scarce, people were on the breadline – you couldn't blame them for looking after their families.'

He has a fund of stories, including the time a well-known runner from Derby took £100 from a bookmaker to throw a race. Lew won't tell me his name in case relatives are still about.

For many years, he performed semi-professionally in a Derby dance band, swam, played bowls, and made his own wine. It's the wine that I remember most. I rarely walked past his house in Harcourt Street without him knocking on the window to invite me in for a tasting. It was good stuff, too. I usually went home slightly more confused then when I'd arrived – 'squiffy', as my dear old Aunt Ivy used to say.

Silver birch sap was a particularly good drink. Or it might have been parsnip and passion fruit. I told you I was confused.

Thirteen years ago, he suffered a mild stroke and his doctor advised him to stop, even though he'd just won a veterans' half-marathon. 'I've been running since my early teens. I can't imagine giving it up,' he told me then. But he accepted the inevitable: 'I suppose, if you have any sense, you follow doctor's orders.'

As Lew says: 'You only get one life and one body – make the most of both.' And coming from a man who didn't run his first marathon until he had passed retirement age, it seems sound advice.

Having said that, if you'll excuse me, I'm now going for that lie down. After I've raised a glass of wine to Lew Patrick. Homemade, of course.

Flying Pickles, Preserved Plums – What a Waste

During the Second World War, a chap called Archibald Brown was fined £4, plus £6 costs, for wasting butter, margarine, cheese, lard, bread, bacon, pickles and preserved plums. His crime? He threw them at his wife.

The solicitor representing the Ministry of Food told the court at Wincanton in Somerset: 'If there is any acrimonious debate in the home, or any breach of connubial bliss, rations must not be used as weapons of war'.

He must have been a nasty piece of work, must Archie. Even allowing that Mrs Brown might have nagged her hubby to distraction, and although it's difficult to imagine what damage any of the missiles would have caused – unless the pickles and preserved plums were still in their jars, of course – there is never any justification for losing your temper to the extent that you would launch your supper at someone.

Which brings me to the point of the story: Brown wasn't charged, as he quite rightly would be today, with assaulting his wife. His offence was one of wasting food.

Sixty-odd years ago, the world was a far less enlightened place. What bothered the courts then wasn't that Mrs Brown was the target of assorted pantry items, but that there was a war on, food was rationed, and doing anything with it – other than eating it – was considered unpatriotic. They even put up posters to that effect.

In the Gerard Street of my childhood, the only real hazard to a game of street football was the pig bin by the lamp-post, six doors from our house, outside what was still referred to as 'the Ship', even though the pub of that name had been converted to a private dwelling during the First World War.

People talk about recycling as though it's a new idea, but during the war, and in the days of rationing that followed, households were encouraged to put their waste food into the public bins that were dotted around every street. The food went for animal feed, hence the name 'pig bin'.

That bin nearest our house also served as a useful wicket for a game of street cricket, until one of us knocked it over that is; then everyone scattered rather than have the responsibility of collecting up the cabbage stalks, potato peelings and other rotting food rubbish that was strewn across the pavement. Arthur Smith, who lived at the Ship house, must have dreaded the light nights.

Whatever, if you lived through food rationing, you will know that those of us of a certain vintage still feel guilty about leaving food uneaten on our plates.

Yet a recent cross-Whitehall study into higher food costs identified waste as a factor. The report said that, each year, British households throw away a total of four million tons of food, worth £1 billion, that could have been eaten.

At that rate, even the generation that was told to eat up everything must now contribute to the nation's overflowing waste bins.

I suppose it has a lot to do with being obsessed by sell-by dates. It used to be so different: if you had to scoop a few lumps of milk off your tea in hot weather . . . well, most of us survived to tell the tale.

All of which reinforces my feeling that Archibald Brown was not a nice person.

My own parents were not averse to the occasional verbal spat around the dinner table. But, even at the height of the stormiest debate, my father never had to be ready to take evasive action in case a jar of pickled walnuts came flying his way.

WHEN CHICKEN WAS ONLY A CHRISTMAS DAY TREAT

It doesn't take much to start a debate in a pub. There I was, sitting in the buzzing Rowditch Inn with my good friend and neighbour, Peter Hampson, when someone said that they enjoyed the previous week's column about the end of food rationing in Britain.

That conversation quickly turned into that old chestnut about the nation being in much better health when one week's post-war food ration for an adult was probably the equivalent of what most of us now eat comfortably in one day.

Peter, who when he isn't keeping me company in pubs, writes a rural affairs column, has definite views on the subject, as I soon discovered.

'People who criticize supermarkets for "ruining" modern food would have a real shock if they were transported back to the 1950s,' he declared.

'There's a lot of sentimental nonsense talked about how food was of a higher quality and more wholesome when it was sold only by the old high street butchers, bakers and greengrocers.

'There were some excellent shops, but you had to pay top prices to enjoy their goods. Today's idea of good food would probably have been beyond the pockets of most people, 50 years ago.'

I agreed, nostalgia merchants overlook the fact that, in those days, many shopkeepers sold low-quality food simply because that was all that most people could afford. Butchers hid large lumps of bone in rolled joints; greengrocers proudly displayed top-grade tomatoes at the front of their counters while selling customers the over-ripe or bruised produce from underneath them.

As Peter said, you have to be from our generation to realize that, in comparative terms, we're confronted by an Aladdin's Cave of nutrition every time we walk into Tesco or Sainsbury's, confronted as we are by a multiplicity of different foodstuffs from all around the world. It is all of general high quality, and sold for relatively low prices. You can travel around the globe at the cheese counter alone, although when I saw Brussels sprouts imported from Australia, I did wonder whether this was the ultimate folly of air-food-miles.

Those who moan about mass production being responsible for reducing flavour are missing the point that, for instance, most people would presumably rather eat chicken regularly than not at all.

Half a century ago, in Derby, chicken was something we saw only on Christmas Day. Peter's boyhood, in Belper, wasn't any different.

'Yes, Christmas – and it was always the old laying hen that had been boiled for a day to tenderize it sufficiently for roasting. We thought it was delicious but, looking back, eating what meat there was left on the carcase was like chewing string.'

It is claimed that former Russian president, Boris Yeltsin, wept when he visited the food hall of an American supermarket for the first time after the collapse of the Soviet Union. The abundance was in sharp contrast to the queues and food shortages that he'd left behind. I can believe that. Back in the 1980s, another journalist friend, the late Geoff Hammerton, entertained a Russian fellow member of the Universal Esperanto Organization. She, too, was reduced to tears by the sight of a British supermarket. And that was only in Mickleover.

The debate on food miles and the like is valid. But it does include a lot of nonsense from people who have only ever known full stomachs.

Four months after this article originally appeared, Peter Hampson died on his 60th birthday, from a brain tumour. It is reprinted here in memory of many wonderful evenings spent in the Rowditch Inn, debating the world with a fine journalist and a good friend.

I Preferred Snooker with Salty the Irishman

It was a photograph, produced by Paul Walton at one of our Friday lunchtime get-togethers, that puzzled us. The personnel were obvious enough – Wally himself, Derek Grantham, John Cheadle and Derek Taylor – and, judging by the suits and haircuts, it was taken in the mid-1960s. But where?

Wally is wearing a carnival mask, so we thought that perhaps it was a New Year's Eve party, in which case it would have to be at the Norman Arms in Village Street, where Redfern Athletic held an annual such do.

That raised a smile. One year, I got the tickets printed by a firm called the Clarion Press on London Road, a one-man band run by a lovely chap called Norman Ray.

When I went to collect the job, Norman looked worried: 'I've been trying to get hold of you. I can't start it yet. You haven't put the date on the copy.'

'Blimey, Norman,' I said, 'it's a New Year's Eve party. How many more clues do you want?'

We had a good chuckle about that.

But this photograph wasn't taken at the Norman. A closer inspection of the fixtures and fittings, plus strangers in the background, ruled it out.

Eventually, we settled on the bowling alley that used to stand in Colyear Street. A lot of the Redfern boys were regulars and John Cheadle thought that the occasion might have been one of the 'birthday parties' held to celebrate another year of ten-pin bowling there.

I was never a patron of the bowling alley myself. I preferred the Regent snooker hall over Abbot's Hill Chambers in Babington Lane. Unlike the 'bowl', the Regent had a delicious seediness about it and the regulars were a real cast of characters; not least Salty, an Irishman who always played snooker in a flat cap and Wellington boots. What an education for a young grammar school boy in the 1950s.

But back to Wally's photograph: he wanted a repeat performance, a matter of some urgency since Derek G was visiting from Australia and it might be some years before everyone in the picture was in Derby again.

The first attempt foundered because John was in Monaco, attending the European Champions' League draw. What a life: I never made it further than the Loco Club in Calvert Street, for the Derby Sunday League Cup draw.

When John returns from these jaunts, he always has a tale to tell. My favourite is the one about meeting Danny DeVito in a hotel lift. This time, he sat next to Eusebio at a dinner.

Anyway, last week, after my favourite travel agent had returned from breaking bread with Benfica's Black Pearl, we reconvened at the Rowditch Inn. There were the quartet in the original picture, plus yours truly who had been elected official photographer for the evening.

'We must recreate it absolutely,' said Derek G, 'so I need a pint glass with a handle.'

'If you're going for an exact re-run,' I said, 'then why haven't you turned up in the same suit and tie? Plus we aren't in a bowling alley.'

In the interests of historical accuracy, Derek T did produce a mask for Wally to wear, but he declined the opportunity to look like Zorro.

Finally Wally announced that his posh digital camera was broken and instead produced one of those disposable jobs that you have to send to Boots.

It's difficult, establishing the same shot when you're squinting through a viewfinder not much bigger than the head of a match. No matter: when the tableau turns out to be less than perfect, I expect I shall still get the blame.

WE'RE ALL AGREED: IT'S DOWNHILL FROM HERE

It came as a complete surprise – the chance to buy a cut-price terracotta rhubarb enforcer. I've never dealt with the company that emailed me. Nevertheless, they were anxious that I should know about their unbeatable offer. It was a tricky moment, too. Until then, I hadn't realized that I might be in the market for such a thing. But you know how it is. You see a bargain and ask yourself: 'Can I really afford not to buy that?'

In the end, I let common sense decide. I'd got gout, so the doc suggested that I lay off best bitter. But, he'd also advised that I lay off rhubarb. And since I'd agreed to meet him halfway – and the Rowditch Inn doesn't sell rhubarb – the temptation to purchase the enforcer, bargain of a lifetime though it may have been, was resisted.

In the meantime (stick with me here; there is a point to all this), according to a study carried out by the University of Derby, most people in their 60th year believe that they have been fortunate to spend their working lives in a period of relatively high prosperity, without the shadow of world wars.

They are, according to Margaret Christopoulos who conducted the survey, the Never Had It So Good generation. So, Harold Macmillan was a prophet after all.

But, never mind Supermac, I could have told her this for nothing. Albeit those funding the university probably insist on such research being carried out scientifically, rather than by simply noting the collective ramblings of some slowly dilapidating Derbeians who, on Friday lunchtimes, gather for a few beers and routinely chunter: 'We're glad we were born when we were. We've had the best of it. It's all downhill now.' It's something on which we all agree.

Of course, the subjects of Ms Christopoulos's research were born in the late 1940s, so most are probably still in gainful employment, whereas the majority of our little group are a bit older, born when Hitler still went to bed dreaming of world domination.

We've all retired from full-time work (otherwise, what would we be doing sitting in a pub all afternoon?), but our perceptions are much the same as those of her study group: being born when we were means that the bulk of our lives have been spent in good times rather than bad.

But what changes we've seen. When I started school in 1950, I was issued with a slate and chalk. The other day, I read that the consensus is that a good age to introduce your child to the computer is – three.

You know, sometimes I wish that the World Wide Web had never been invented. It makes research and communication so much more accessible, but internet addiction can also spoil lives. It's so very easy to spend hours on a computer, mindlessly surfing, instead of reading a book, talking to friends, listening to music, or going for a walk.

And here lies my point: never mind the good old days, us 60-somethings often find the 21st century's information super highway utterly bewildering.

I keep getting emails from someone, a woman I assume, called Brittany Ferries, trying to sell me trips to France. Then there is the persistent suggestion from a social networking site that I should make a friend of Sinharaja Rain Forest, whoever he is.

And how on earth do you become a target for the purveyors of terracotta rhubarb enforcers? How many others have been selected?

Maybe I should ask the university to carry out a survey. Better yet, I'll enquire down at the pub.

STATE PENSION? RING BACK IN TWO MONTHS' TIME

It was the letter for which I had been waiting. The one from the Department of Work and Pensions, headed: 'Claim Your State Pension'. And it looked simple, too. No form to complete. You just rang a number, and away you went. Well, not quite. I should have listened to my pal. His pension is due in September, three months before mine. So he'd already received his letter.

'Don't waste your time,' he advised, giving a passable impression of that Johnny Knowall character in the Al Read wireless show (apologies to anyone under 50, but the Salford sausage maker turned comedy king was one of my heroes).

'When you ring,' my pal continued, 'all you'll get is a recorded announcement telling you to ring again in two months' time. And, by the way, when you do ring again in two months' time – you'll find that they've changed the number.'

'Well,' I said, '"that was three months ago. So I think I will ring, like it says. They've probably sorted it by now.' And I did. And, of course, they hadn't.

Instead, I also got a recorded announcement telling me to ring again in two months' time. And when I do, I expect I'll get another recorded message, telling me that they've changed the number. Just like my pal predicted.

The reason they gave for me calling back later is that they've 'improved our system'. I wanted to say that it's not much of an improvement if they're still sending out letters encouraging would-be pensioners to make pointless telephone calls. But, of course, you never get to speak to a real human being. The DWP don't want you doing that.

Just like supermarkets don't want you bothering checkout operators when you can do the job for them. And just like banks don't want you speaking to a counter clerk when you can pay into a machine instead.

It's a worrying trend that has been extended even to the NHS. We've already got a self-service check-in system, and I've joked about self-service triage being next. But I never thought I'd see a sign on a surgery door that effectively said: 'If you're ill, go away.'

There it was, though, big and bold, at the height of the swine flu scare. It gave a number to ring, of course. Then a 16-year-old with one hour's training could diagnose you over the phone. So that probably doesn't count as self-service, although it must be the next-best thing.

We've gone a long way backwards since I lined up with my old granny in the pension queue at Abbey Street post office (that's gone, along with every other sub-post office within walking distance), inhaling the Sloan's Liniment and mothballed fox furs of a dozen similar grannies. It was the highlight of her week. And mine, too, if she bought me a toy.

Those were the days when banks were managed by Mr Mainwaring characters, and staffed by flesh and blood, not machines (nowadays, the only breathing bank staff you're likely to encounter are those prowling queues, peddling insurance). When shopkeepers were pleased to talk to customers. And when, even at the height of a nationwide polio scare, doctors' surgeries didn't put up the barricades.

Of course, you'll say that I'm just getting old. And you're right. But grumbling is one of the perks of advancing years. And the sudden realization that you'll soon be 65 brings life into sharper focus. Somehow, it's fulfilling to join in with the chuntering.

Do you know what? I think I'm ready to become a pensioner. Provided I can remember to ring back in two months' time.

BOWLING ALONG TO FIND THE SPORT FOR ME

The Travel Agent raised an interesting point: 'Have you ever wondered, Rip, if there is something that you'd have been world-class at, if only you'd got round to trying it?'

He's been calling me 'Rip' ever since we were at school. Once he rang BBC Radio Derby and asked for a record request for the two of us, purely to publicize a charity football match that we were organizing. They played it. But the presenter thought I was the Cheadles' pet dog. And although I can take a ribbing, a month of being asked if I wanted to go for walkies did begin to wear a bit thin. Not to mention the lamp-post jokes.

Anyway, back to the point. The man who used to take Liverpool FC on their European travels hasn't suddenly become a philosopher in his golden years. What prompted him to raise that intriguing point was my own musing over whether – in the year in which you are due to collect your old-age pension – it is still possible to find a sport at which you can truly excel.

It was the topic of crown green bowls that had led us here. Just lately, Friday lunchtimes seem to be dominated by talk of roll-ups, and touchers, and dead ends, and re-spotted jacks. And there's nothing worse than being in the middle of a conversation when you're the only person who hasn't a clue as to what everyone else is talking about.

So, after a few weeks, I tried to join in. I just came out with it: 'Did you know that the world's oldest surviving bowling green is the Southampton Old Bowling Green, which was first used in 1299?'

Disappointingly, there were no takers for that nugget of bowls information, mined from Wikipedia just before I set off for the pub. Instead, a discussion erupted about the merits of something called Lignum Vitae, which I assumed was a health drink (don't write in; I now know that it's some kind of wood).

I tried again: 'Did you also know that an Act of Parliament of

1541 – which was not repealed until 1845 – ruled that artificers, labourers, apprentices, servants and the like were forbidden to play bowls at any time except Christmas, and then only in their master's house and presence? Or else they got fined 6s 8d.'

Again, there wasn't a flicker. So I feigned an interest in playing the game myself, just to get some attention.

'You never know,' I said, 'this could be the sport I'm good at.'

Because although I played Sunday football (mainly lumbering around at full-back, dealing out gravel rash to adventurous wingers), and turned my arm over for Derby Red Rose 2nd XI in friendly cricket, when it comes to sporting excellence, I've always been an also-ran.

So I knew where the Travel Agent was coming from when he confirmed the intriguing possibility that gold-medal potential at a hitherto untried sport may lurk under this stiff-jointed exterior.

'I don't think it would actually be crown green bowls,' I said. 'My hand-to-eye co-ordination is poor. It's all to do with my left eyeball. The optician at Boots says it's shaped like a rugby ball instead of a football.'

The Travel Agent warmed to his theme: 'Well, let's think again. It obviously couldn't be anything to do with running.'

'Agreed,' I said.

'I know,' he said, 'have you thought about bobsledding?'

Then Wilf chipped in: 'Did you know that bobsledding was invented by an Englishman?' He's obviously been at Wikipedia, too.

By now, though, I'd completely lost interest. If you can't be serious for five minutes . . .

WHERE THE CUSTOMER IS NEVER RIGHT

We should have guessed immediately that there were going to be difficulties. It was like this: we were half an hour early – you have to build in possible delays when travelling by taxi – and it was raining heavily; the pub across the road looked pretty full (they were showing a televised football match). And that was why we went straight into the restaurant, a few miles south of Derby.

From the moment we entered, the signs weren't good. The surly young lass who unlocked the door for us looked mightily put out. And so did the woman who arrived hot on the girl's heels. If we were expecting a smile to brighten up the grey day, we were going to be disappointed.

'You're not supposed to be here yet,' the woman told us sniffily.

'Well, it's either that or walk round in the rain,' our Nicola told her. 'So, we hoped you wouldn't mind.'

She made it clear that she did mind. And she also minded later, when she discovered that we were 'The Vegetarians' whose presence had apparently caused the chef to prepare a special meal for people beamed down from another planet.

Or – worse even that that – not proper vegetarians at all. Not humanoids that eschewed all flesh. But awkward blighters who still ate fish. And who wanted to do so today. There is a word for us and I think it is 'pescatarians'. Although as far as the proprietor here was concerned, it appeared that 'pains in the backside' was a more appropriate description.

I tried to sympathize. I mean, just think: people wanting to come into the warmth of your restaurant rather than spend 30 minutes of a cold Sunday teatime standing outside in teeming rain.

And then, when you discover that these are the ones you've been told don't eat meat. Well, the blighters turn the job on its head and each order the fish dish. Clearly, 'The Customer Is Always Right' is not a motto that hangs in the staff room of this particular establishment.

It was awkward. We were someone else's guests. And the food, when it arrived, was excellent, albeit there were a few adventures with bacon and chicken appearing in the middle of vegetarian starters (well, if vegetarians start dabbling with fish, what can they expect?).

In fact, it was the loveliest occasion with the nicest people you'll meet. And I doubt that anyone who turned up spot-on the appointed time, and who didn't mess the boss about by deciding to eat fish, would have said that it was anything other than a perfect evening. Me? Well, I wouldn't let a grumpy restaurateur dampen my spirits. I had a great time too.

So why mention it? Well, to illustrate something that I have long believed: when it comes to restaurant service, nobody does it better than foreigners.

It wasn't a coincidence that the members of staff who proved charming and attentive throughout the other evening weren't British. I don't know where they came from. Somewhere in Eastern Europe, I would guess. Wherever, they deserve great credit.

In 1907, a publication called *The London Truth* told its readers: 'It is often a matter of wonder why foreign waiters are preferred to English ones, even in English hotels. The reason is very simple: the foreigner is a far better waiter.'

The problem may be that British diners don't always value waiting staff, whereas in almost every other part of the world, people respect those who serve them.

So, like the woman the other evening implied: it was probably all my fault anyway.

HERE'S A TIP: GIVE US A SMILE

It was a pleasant late spring Sunday morning on Darley Park. The sun was shining and it was crowded. There were young couples hand-in-hand, older people with their grandchildren, locals exercising their dogs. On the rugby field, schoolboys were training. We'd walked from the city centre, through Darley Fields, pausing to watch the canoeists at Darley Abbey before strolling into the park itself. And we were ready for a cuppa.

It was while queuing in the park cafe that I spotted it: a receptacle on the counter, with a sign soliciting tips. It struck me as odd. Why would you want to tip someone whose only function had been to pour you a cup of tea and place it before you? It must have taken all of 30 seconds and I reflected on what was the going rate for such a simple service.

I was going to be smart and say to the girl who served me that I would give her two tips: 'Always make eye contact with your customers. And, if possible, try to conjure up a smile.'

But, as I've said before, Mrs R objects to my making a public fuss when she is present. So I set aside the idea, gathered up our drinks and made for a vacant table.

There, I launched into one of my hobby horses (Mrs R has heard it all before, so she was only pretending to listen): the whole subject of tipping. And I always begin with the same story.

I was having lunch with John Pawsey, my agent for 30 years, in London, in Simpson's in the Strand to be precise. It was my turn to pay and, when the waiter came with his credit card machine – this was in the days before chip and pin – inevitably there was a space for a gratuity. So I added 10 per cent.

On the train back to Derby, I was sorting out my paperwork when I came across the bill again. And this time I noticed that a 12.5 per cent 'discretionary' service charge had already been added. So I'd tipped them twice.

You're right: I should have studied the bill properly first time round. But it had been a long lunch. And, anyway, when you're invited to add a gratuity, you assume that the establishment hasn't already done so.

I should say that this was several years ago and is no reflection on the people who currently run Simpson's. But it left me questioning the whole practice of tipping. For instance, a tip is based on a percentage of the total bill. So explain to me why I should tip more for a waiter to bring me a £50 bottle of wine (not that I've ever spent that much on wine), than if he'd carried over a £15 bottle?

Nowadays, I never add a tip to a restaurant bill – who knows who's getting it anyway? – although I'm happy to hand over a fiver direct to a waiter or waitress if they've contributed something more to my restaurant experience than simply delivering food to my table without a scowl on their face.

Amazingly, considering that, these days, US waiting staff literally demand tips, in 1904, the Anti-Tipping Society of America sprang up in Georgia, its 100,000 members signing pledges not to tip anyone for a year.

In the 19th century, the Scottish writer, Thomas Carlyle, after leaving the Bell Inn in Gloucester, complained: 'The dirty scrub of a waiter grumbled about his allowance, which I reckoned liberal. I added sixpence to it, and [he] produced a bow, which I was near rewarding with a kick.'

That might be taking it too far.

I Wish MPs' Gravy Train Had Stopped Here

It's a few years since we've had the eaves on the side of our house painted. At one time they were done regularly, every time the rest of the exterior was spruced up, in fact. Then Health and Safety intervened. It's like this. In the old days, our regular painter used to nip up his ladder, slap on some trade exterior, and 10 minutes later we were good for another five years.

Then one day, when he was pricing up the job, he produced a particularly sharp intake of breath. And started talking about scaffolding. It appeared that, although you rarely read about professional painters falling off ladders (in fact, I Googled the topic and came up with zero examples), Health and Safety now insisted on scaffolding being erected in certain conditions. And the painting of our eaves fell slap bang in the middle of them.

So, as the cost of hiring scaffolding was many hundreds of pounds more than the cost of the paint job itself – we are talking about only a few square feet of wood here – we decided to leave our eaves as they were. And so they have remained ever since. Because, being members of the general public, we cannot really justify the cost of doing otherwise.

Which brings me to my point. I was relating this story to my pal, Alf, down at the Rowditch Inn and he came up with a foolproof way of getting the eaves painted at absolutely no cost to myself whatsoever.

And not just the eaves. The whole house, inside and out, too. And getting the garden sorted. And the weekly shopping bill, including cat food for two perpetually hungry moggies. And, if we possessed any, all the chandeliers in Rippon Folly cleaned regularly. In fact, Alf's list was endless.

His cunning plan that would allow me to enjoy all this? Get myself elected to Parliament.

'It's simple,' said Alf, 'just become an MP, and then the world will be your oyster. Just think, you could even buy a holiday cottage and nominate it as your second home.'

I had to bring him down the earth.

'Nice idea, Alf,' I said. 'But it's too late. They've all been rumbled. Even our local representative is going to have to fork out for her own hanging baskets in future.'

So, I've missed the boat – or in this case the gravy train – again. Alf's suggestion did, however, stimulate a wider debate on the whys and wherefores of the recent furore over MPs' expenses. For a start, why pick out Tory toffs for special vilification? Are their sharp practices any worse than those of some New Labourite who's also never had a proper job?

What is the difference between Sir Bartley Humbug-Fotheringstall having the taxpayer cough up for new chains to his drawbridge, and Bert Figgis slipping through a flat-screen telly on which to view adult films (rented at the public's expense, of course)?

'The thing is,' said Alf, 'that everyone's at it. It's not just MPs. Expenses fiddling is rife everywhere.'

'True,' I said, 'but not to this degree. And besides, it's surely not naive to think that MPs, of all people, should be beyond reproach.'

Actually, it is ironic that a newspaper should bring this matter to the public's attention. Because in the old days, a journalist's expenses were notoriously a work of fiction.

In Derby, there was one marvellous character that proved outstandingly inventive when it came to 'doing his exes'. One day he claimed the cost of drinks for 'counselling a prostitute' in the Globe in Irongate. Unlike our elected leaders, I don't think he got away with it.

ETIQUETTE DILEMMA POSED BY MOBILE PHONES

It was a tricky one. I was on a train to London and there was the usual babble of people on mobile phones. All trying to show each other how dynamic they were. Which was a pretty pointless exercise since everyone was doing the same thing. So there was no real audience. Except for me. And I'm not easily impressed. Not that the rest of them knew that.

Anyway, the chap sitting opposite me had rung someone up to find out the date of an apparently important meeting. And if he said: 'Right, Friday. Oh sorry, yes, Thursday . . . ' once, then he must have said it half a dozen times.

And all the time, I was sitting there, trying to concentrate on the crossword, but thinking: 'How many more times does he need to be told?'

Eventually, he rang off. Whereupon I offered up a silent prayer of thanks – well, I muttered it actually, just to make a point – before returning to the seemingly insurmountable problem of 18 across.

But before I could refocus, the man dialled someone else. And then told them that the meeting was on – Friday. I couldn't believe it.

I'm sitting there, desperately wanting to lean across, tap him on the arm, and say: 'No, you've got it wrong again. It's Thursday.'

And that was my dilemma. What, by the wildest stretch of the imagination, had it got to do with me?

So I said nothing. I just spent the rest of the journey wondering whether I should. Obviously, the person he'd called was going to miss the meeting. But what could I do? I wish there was a book about mobile phone etiquette to help you decide when it's OK to intervene in something that's none of your business.

Talking about mobile phone books, my friend Andy Ward and I once wrote one about all the daft one-sided conversations to which we'd been privy.

You'd like Andy. He's an Old Bemrosian and his dad, Tim, used to pay for and manage the Rams. We've collaborated on a few, but the mobile phone one was one of the most enjoyable to put together. We spent about a year collecting the stories. We eavesdropped on trains, in shopping malls, in pubs and on street corners. Once I was overhearing so many mobile phone conversations at once that I couldn't hear the one next to me for the one three tables away.

And as Andy observed, we realized that we were capturing a slice of social history. Mobiles brought a new style of conversation, with their excessive turn-taking and need to define geographical location ('I'm on the train' being the most annoying).

Our favourite was the man sitting opposite three strangers in a railway carriage. He calls his girlfriend and arranges to meet her that evening.

Then he rings his wife and tells her that he is working late and will have to stay over in a hotel. Then he goes to the buffet car, leaving his phone on the table.

The others look at each other uneasily. Finally, one of them, a young woman, picks up the phone and redials the last number: 'Look, you don't know me but I'm on a train and just heard your husband make his last two calls. He isn't working tonight. He's meeting his girlfriend.'

The woman puts the phone back and says to the man next to her: 'Do you think I did the right thing?'

'No,' he says. 'But if you ever want a job, just give me your name and address.'

And I should worry about someone missing a meeting?

It's Too Dynamically Stable to Snow, Apparently

The man at the bar was adamant: it was too cold to snow. Then look what happened. Before you could say 'Jack Frost' everywhere was covered in a white blanket. Too cold to snow? How can it be too cold to snow? It's a jolly sight colder at the North Pole and it snows there. And down at the other end of the planet, penguins always look to be shivering as they shuffle over several feet of the stuff. I bet if penguins had teeth, they'd be permanently chattering

Too cold to snow – it's just one of those clichés that people trot out. And it annoys me. So I resolved that, when I got home, I would check out the veracity of the statement and then, next time someone said that it was too cold to snow, I'd have an answer.

The internet was the obvious place to look and, sure enough, if you Google 'too cold to snow', no less than 51,500 web pages clamour for your attention.

I tried the first in line, a weather prediction site where meteorologist Jeff Harby backed me up.

'In actuality, earth's troposphere is not too cold to snow but rather it is "too dynamically stable to snow"' writes Jeff (he's American, obviously).

That stopped me in my tracks. Now I needed to know what 'troposphere' meant, but I couldn't be bothered to go off at a tangent. That's the trouble with the internet. You start off looking to see if it really can be too cold to snow and five hours later you're reading up about the art of pen-spinning in Western Samoa.

Anyway, the next time someone tells me that it's too cold to snow, I'll say airily: 'Well, actually, it's too dynamically stable to snow.' I'll be all right as long as they don't want me to explain it.

In the meantime, I have a few other hobby horses about snow, the main one being that I don't see why the whole country now thinks it's OK to take a day off at the first sign of a few flakes.

One Friday afternoon in February 1969, it snowed so heavily that the Blue Bus on which I was travelling home that evening got stuck in Doles Lane and I walked the five miles from Findern back to our house in Young Street in New Normanton through huge snowdrifts. At one point traffic was at a standstill in one long line from Littleover back to Lichfield.

I got home about 10 o'clock that night and – no mobile phones in those days – the heavily pregnant Mrs R was beginning to wonder if I'd stopped for a pint and was tucked up in a cosy pub, or whether I was lying out in a field somewhere about to expire from hypothermia (her money was firmly on the first scenario, so she didn't bother to phone the police).

The point is that I was still back at the *Derby Telegraph*'s Burton office at nine o'clock the next morning. Not to turn up would have been unthinkable. I just got up extra early, stood shivering at the bus stop for about an hour, and eventually the good old Blue Bus turned up and I was still at my desk by the appointed time.

Nowadays, the country's gone soft. I don't ever remember missing a day's work or being given a day off school just because it had snowed.

Of course, the problem might be that, until last week, we hadn't had a decent snowfall for years.

As the man at the bar might say – we're just not used to it.

'HAVE YOU EVER BEEN A CIRCUS PERFORMER?'

A question: you've gone into a bank to enquire about opening a small deposit account. So do you expect to be asked if you've ever dabbled in sword swallowing or lion taming? I'll explain. When a financial maelstrom recently threatened to swallow the developed world, and economic Armageddon appeared nigh, Mrs R and me thought it prudent to spread our ever-dwindling funds around a bit.

It seemed a straight-forward operation: you enter one of the high street banks in Derby, offer to lodge a few quid with it, and, a few minutes later, you're walking out with the paperwork done.

And in the days when banks operated on a very simple premise – you lent them money and they lent that to other people, pocketing the small difference in interest rates for a fair profit – that was about all there was to it.

But long gone are the days when banks employed managers of the Mr Mainwaring ilk. Now they've closed down most of the tills, expect you to pay in at machines – rather like Tesco and Sainsbury's encourage their customers to perform as unpaid checkout operators – and then patrol the resultant queues trying to sell you services you don't want.

So it was in our bank of choice the other week. We were offered everything from life insurance to health insurance, from the Super Platinum Premier Plus current account (main attraction being free roadside recovery, which isn't much of an attraction at all to a man who has never bothered to learn to drive a motor vehicle) to the Diamond Supreme Double Premier Plus account, which offers an interest rate a tad above the minuscule one generally available, the only drawback being that you have to keep it topped up with a sum equivalent to the GDP of a small African nation.

I'm the last man in the world to fall for any kind of sell, hard or soft.

But when the bank person asked me about house insurance, even I thought it worth a look. These are hard times and the saving of a few bob here and there isn't to be sniffed at.

Of course, before a quotation could be given there was a form to be completed. This started off predictably enough – name, address, type of building to be insured, number of bedrooms, and so on – but the next question floored me: 'Are you, or have you ever been, a circus performer?'

Under all normal circumstances I would have wanted to know why that was relevant. Indeed, I would have made a meal of it. But Mrs R was sitting next to me and she doesn't like me making a fool of myself in public, at least not when she is present.

So even though, this time, I definitely heard her stifle a chuckle, I just said something about not moving my circus career forward because I kept falling off the tightrope, and we proceeded to more mundane matters like burglar alarms and smoke detectors.

As it happened, the bank's quotation was a bit cheaper than the company we'd been using, but as we emerged into some rare sunshine on St Peter's Street, this circus business was still bothering me.

'Why on earth did she ask me about circus performing?' I asked, as we made our way to coffee.

'Maybe,' said Mrs R, 'if you'd said yes, then you'd have had to specify what you did. They're probably worried about fire-eaters practising in their sitting rooms.'

'But there must be lots of dangerous pursuits you could carry out at home,' I argued, 'so why pick on circus performers?'

It is a puzzle, to be sure.

CYCLISTS' RIGHT OF WAY – THEY TAKE IT ANYWAY

It had been a while since I'd last set eyes on Mick Mullinger. I was waiting at a bus stop on Mansfield Road when he pulled up in his car to offer me a lift. Or maybe he was already on the bus when I boarded. No, come to think of it, I was walking through the Westfield Centre and he was also threading his way through the crowd, looking like a man on a mission. So it was probably Christmas and he was present hunting.

Whatever, an email from Mick Mull pinged into my in-box. It had occurred to him that we hadn't seen each other for ages, so he thought he'd get in touch for a grumble. That's the wonderful thing about email: it's the pizza of the communications world. A full-blown dinner date normally carries with it expectations; a quick pizza has no strings attached. So it is with emails.

Not that Mick would ever invite me to dinner, you understand. True, I've known him since we were at Bemrose School, and he was always a genial companion down the pub. But here I'm simply drawing an analogy. For a quick hello, emails are just perfect. Phone calls can't normally be just be a two-minute affair; you have to thrash around for things to say, drumming up small talk to make the whole exercise seem worthwhile.

Although on this occasion, Mick was far from short of words. And when it comes to being baffled by modern life, it seems that we are indeed two peas from the same pod.

For instance, like me, Mick was astounded by the recent story of a Devon lifeboat crew who saved a drowning girl but, three hours later, had their inflatable craft confiscated by the Health and Safety zealots.

Apparently it had been taken out of service in June because of a defective hull, but the crew had raised £2,000 to have it repaired and were merely awaiting an inspection when the emergency call came in.

As the girl in distress was only 150 yards out to sea, and the nearest lifeboat six miles away, it seemed a good idea to disregard the red tape. Now, however, they face disciplinary action from the Maritime and Coastguard Agency.

'What a country,' said Mick. 'Save a life and risk your job.'

Actually, they were all volunteers, which somehow makes the situation even more of a nonsense.

Poor old Mick: twice this year, he's been hit by pavement cyclists in Derby, and while he acknowledged that roads are undoubtedly dangerous places for people on bikes, I presume he had his tongue wedged firmly in his cheek when he suggested that we may as well pass a new bylaw giving cyclists the right of way on all footpaths, shopping centres, river banks and the main corridors of the Royal Derby Hospital.

Yet, maybe even that isn't in the realms of fantasy. The other day, a health professional parked her car at the bottom of our street. As I passed her on my way to the bus stop, she was rummaging about in the vehicle's boot.

A few moments later, she brushed past me, riding one of those collapsible bicycles. I watched her pedalling merrily off into the distance – on the pavement all the way to the Royal Derby.

The authorities there apparently encourage staff to arrive either on foot or by bike, but I assume the intention isn't to get them to park their cars in nearby streets and then use the footpath to cycle the last few hundred yards. I might pose the question. By email, of course.

ALTERNATIVE COMEDIANS? WHAT IS THE ALTERNATIVE?

It was Wally who brought up the subject of comedians. Or at least the fact that nowadays – Peter Kay excepted – there don't appear to be any; none worthy of the description at any rate. We were sitting in the pub when the debate erupted. That's not Wally's real name, by the way; it's Paul Walton but, like almost every member of Redfern Athletic back in the 1960s, he was known by his nickname rather than his real moniker.

Take Jack Dobson: sometimes he was known as Ronnie, which was doubly confusing since Jack wasn't his real name either; it was Alan. Derek Grantham was always Vince because we once played a team from Grantham called St Vincent's.

For reasons that cannot be divulged here, Derek Taylor was universally known as Ted. Incidentally, he lived at Etwall where his father kept pigs. Derek always claimed they were racing pigs, but I never really believed him.

Barry Williamson was always Wilf, although apparently no one knew why. And because he'd been to university, Dave Tretton always had to answer to Bamber, as in Gascoigne of *University Challenge* fame. In those days, few people aspired to university; we just got jobs at 16 years of age.

Dave and Barry, or Bamber and Wilf, were a comedy act on their own. On one pre-season tour, in the attic of their bedroom in an ancient Belgian hotel, they found a set of musical instruments. With the aid of a dusty tuba, in the small hours of the morning they produced a ghostly sound to awaken the players in the room directly below.

Then they decided to knock on the door. The idea was that someone would open it to be confronted by a real-life spook. Dave threw a sheet over Barry's head, but the plan dissolved when he was guiding him down the darkened corridor and a small German boy came around the corner on his way to the lavatory (this was definitely a non-en-suite establishment).

He froze in terror, and I don't suppose that Dave assuring him: 'It's all right, it's only Wilf,' was much comfort to the little lad.

But back to comedians, or rather the lack of them. The topic came up after I'd asked if anyone had seen the devastation at Derby Hippodrome.

'What a tragedy,' I said. 'I looked at that stage the other day and thought of all those great radio comics I'd seen there.'

That is what got us started. And where Wally – many Derbeians will remember his parents who ran a newsagent's in Stenson Road – declared that there are no longer any good comedians. We all agreed.

From the old days, Al Read was probably our favourite because his was truly observational comedy. Which is why we voted Peter Kay the only decent modern funny man.

There is nothing more likely to make you laugh than the recognition of a situation, be it Read's tussles with his Johnny Knowall character, or Kay's family wedding routine.

Great comics like Albert Modley, Jimmy James, Tommy Trinder, Ted Ray, Ken Platt and Jimmy Wheeler had honed their acts through thousands of nights on the provincial stage. The 1970s crop that, for years, plied their trade on the club circuit before getting a TV break were also in a different class to today's so-called comedians.

Some years ago, I had the enjoyable experience of working with Max Bygraves on his autobiography. One day we were chatting and I said that I didn't find 'alternative' comedians at all funny.

'Well,' said Max, 'when you think about it, what it the alternative to comedy?'

I reckon he would have liked Wilf and Bamber.

WELL, I'D NEVER HEARD OF JODIE KIDD

So, that's another sporting occasion ticked off my list of things to do before I fall off the perch: a day out at Silverstone for the Formula 1 Grand Prix. Not that I'm particularly interested in motor sport. But there was Lewis Hamilton to cheer on. And, like the Grand National, the Boat Race, Henley Regatta and Wimbledon, the F1 Grand Prix is one of those British institutions that are markers in the passing of another year.

It was just a pity that they didn't make the announcement earlier. Then I could have waited until 2010 and just nipped down the road to Donington Park.

But Formula 1: I'm old enough to remember when Derby's Reg Parnell was a name in the sport; and there has always been something glamorous about the whole F1 tour, with its exotic locations from Monte Carlo to Montreal, Singapore to Sao Paulo.

Not that Silverstone is exotic. It seems to be set down a farm track in the middle of nowhere. And, in truth, if you want to be constantly informed, you'd be better off watching the whole thing on telly with your feet up and a bag of toffee.

Staring at a stretch of bare tarmac every other 90 seconds, with a few seconds of 'vroom, vroom' in between, you've no idea what's going on. And I've only just got my full hearing restored.

No, for me the best part of the day came before the race had even started. I don't spend many Sunday lunchtimes feeling slightly squiffy from too much champagne, watching the Red Arrows swoop between the treetops while I'm chomping on my asparagus.

And there was also a super model. I'd never actually heard of her (but, then again, I once asked Nicole Kidman to shift her bag so I could get past and I'd no idea who she was either).

This girl at Silverstone was called Jodie Kidd: very tall; very posh; and, apparently, very famous. So, emboldened by a few glasses of Laurent Perrier's finest, I decided to get her autograph for my mate

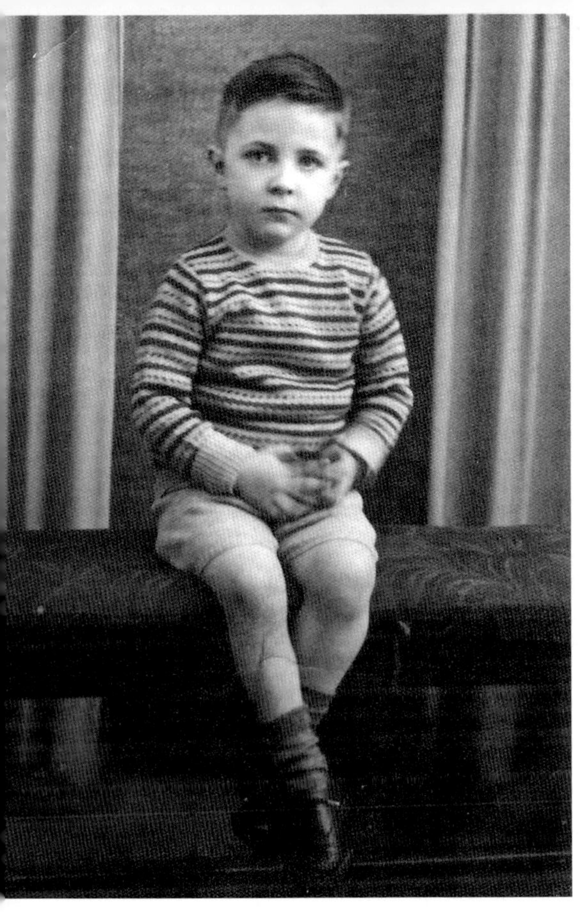

Every Derby child seemed to have their photograph taken at Jerome's studio in Victoria Street. I was no exception. The year was 1950.

Gerard Street shortly before most of these houses were demolished. The house where I was born, at the far end of the row on the left, is still standing, though. The brewery sign of the now demolished Marquis of Granby pub can be seen on the right.

By 1979, Becket School in Gerard Street was awaiting demolition. The front walls had already disappeared to make way for car parking, their iron railings having been removed during the Second World War.

My mother and father at Skegness in 1954. I'm lagging behind somewhere.

You can't get much further from the sea than Derby, but in 1951 we went to Hunstanton. The Golden Age of Steam? Trains were generally dirty and noisy.

Gerard Street–Wilson Street junction in 1979. The former Brewin's newsagent's stands on the far corner. Phil Vidofsky's barber's shop is on the near corner. The same Gerard Street–Wilson Street junction in 2010, flattened to make way for more of Derby's inner ring road.

Tatler's printing works in Abbey Street are still standing but these little terraced houses were demolished to make way for an extension to the works.

The Bedford Arms in Bedford Street, one back-street Derby pub that has so far survived the developers and the downturn in the pub trade.

The Roebuck at the top of Stockbrook Street did not escape the wrecking ball.

Al James's Joke Shop in Monk Street was a
great place for Derby's schoolboys in the 1950s.
The area is now much changed, thanks to work
on the inner ring road.

The railway bridge over the River Derwent
near City Road. It was one of my father's
favourite walks into Darley Park. The line
closed in the 1960s.

Babington Lane in 1954, one Derby view that has not much changed.

Derby Borough fire station in Jury Street in the 1950s. Watching Sunday afternoon fire drills was one way for a small boy to pass his time. A car park now stands here.

A view up Irongate in the 1950s. Apart from pedestrianization and the changing businesses, it is another of the few Derby scenes to have remained largely unchanged. Oh, and the trolley bus wires have gone.

Looking down Irongate in the 1950s. The draper's shop belonged to the family of TV personality, Ted Moult.

Not a pet parrot in sight. Interviewing Derby County's 1946 FA Cup winner, Dally Duncan, at his home in Brighton in 1984, in preparation for a documentary series for BBC Radio Derby.

I am probably telling Bert Mozley that I've never seen a ghost in Friar Gate. The year is 1983 and Bert, who played for Derby County and England, was on a visit from Canada where he had lived since 1955.

Colin, and very charming she was too.

As she was personalizing her picture for him, it did occur to me to ask her to add, just for a joke: 'Thanks for everything.' Or even: 'What a night.'

But then you think: well she doesn't want him suing her for breach of promise one day, and producing this signed postcard as damning evidence that they once had more than a passing acquaintanceship. Of course, he's not that sort of chap. But she didn't know that. So I settled for: 'To Colin, with love, from Jodie.'

When I presented it to him, I got the distinct impression that he'd never heard of her either. Well, we're just two simple lads from Gerard Street, Derby. What would we know about super models?

It's a funny thing, this celebrity business. I was once at a charity dinner and someone behind me kept banging into my chair. Eventually, I got fed up and swung round to give them a piece of my mind. When I saw it was Frank Bruno, I asked him for his autograph, too.

I got back from Silverstone in time to see the end of the tennis (not that I'm interested in that either, but I wanted to see the Swiss bloke with no personality get his come-uppance). And so he did, just. What with a Wimbledon champ and winning Euro 08, the Spanish must be in a right old sporting frenzy. Maybe now they'll finally give up bullfighting.

Note: Of course, Donington Park failed in its bid to stage F1.

KEEP YOUR EYES ON THOSE PRIDE PARK AMERICANS

So, the Americans have taken over at Pride Park. Did I ever tell you about the time I had breakfast with Hillary Clinton? It was a book launch in Chicago and there was Hillary and me, and a few others. Actually, there several hundred others, plus the Secret Service keeping the rest of us a lot more than an arm's length at bay.

But I got close enough to Mrs C to be able report back to Mrs R and daughter, Nicola. I knew what they'd ask me: 'What was she wearing?' So I made notes, which alarmed the woman sitting next to me, who was on the point of calling over the FBI until I explained why I was noting down the colour of the First Lady's frock.

It tickled me that there I was, a lad from Gerard Street, munching cream-cheese bagels and drinking coffee with the wife of the leader of the free world. Later, much later, I found myself hoping that Hillary would emerge as the Democrats' candidate ahead of Obama. If only so that I'd be one step nearer to racking my boast up to: 'Did I ever tell you about the time I had breakfast with a future president of the United States?'

One of my favourite Americans is Tony Bartoli, a New York songwriter. He told me: 'I plan to start a pop group of retirees. I might call it Geriatric and the Pacemakers.'

Tony is self-effacing, but Americans can be full of their own importance (their baseball championship is called the World Series, but the only other country they invite is Canada).

For the best part of a decade I travelled to the States regularly, for pleasure and business. I had a stake in a sports publishing company in New Jersey and, one evening, we were dining at the Peacock Tavern in Princeton when our American managing editor got involved in a long-winded debate about the style in which some scallops might be cooked.

Eventually, the despairing waiter said: 'Madam, as you are displaying a certain amount of trepidation towards the scallops, might I steer you gently in the general direction of the prawns?' I laughed so much that beer came down my nose.

They take their politics seriously, too. One October evening, Mrs R and me were sitting in our favourite bar, the Last Hurrah in Boston. A vice-presidential debate was being shown live on the telly in the corner and, thinking that, back home, someone would just have shouted: 'Switch that so-and-so thing off!' we carried on chatting. Until we realized that people were scowling at us, and urging: 'Sshhh!'

The Last Hurrah was part of the old Parker House Hotel, where JFK announced his plans to run for president. Ho Chi Minh cleared tables there; Malcolm X was a waiter. John Wilkes Booth was there the week before he shot Abraham Lincoln. Just across the road, the King's Chapel commemorates Derby-born Kirk Boott Jnr, a 19th-century American merchant. A cosy, below-street-level venue that served good food and good beer (for America, anyway), the Last Hurrah was steeped in history; my kind of place.

Then, one day, I descended the steps and, horror of horrors, the old brown bar had gone. In its stead, breathless businessmen pumped iron, sweated in rowing machines. My previous visit really had been my Last Hurrah – they'd turned my favourite watering hole into a fitness club. So, keep an eye on these Pride Park Americans, I say. Otherwise, one day, you'll go down to the Rowditch Inn, for a quiet pint in convivial surroundings, and find it's been turned into a health spa.

SEEKING FRESH AIR? TAKE REFUGE IN A PUB

I wonder what Cousin Fred would make of it all. The sun was over the yardarm and a pint in Ye Olde Spa Inn beckoned. It was a nice day, so I took my drink outside. A minute later I was back at the bar, driven from the pub garden by tobacco smoke. It's two years since it became illegal to smoke in an enclosed space in England.

When they passed that law, I bet they didn't realize that non-smokers would eventually have to take refuge in pubs. Cousin Fred, who liked a smoke, would have been puzzled by that.

Actually, Fred 'Soldier' Densham was my second cousin, and

quite a character. He spent four years of the First World War as a prisoner of the Kaiser, and then went off to run a rubber plantation, volunteered again, and ended up spending another four years behind wire, this time in Changi after the Japanese invaded Malaya.

Between the wars, he often came back to Derby, staying at the tobacconist's shop that my grandmother ran in Abbey Street. Ye Olde Spa was just up the road, so he would probably have popped in for a snifter, because Fred also liked a drink. Indeed, until his death in 1972, he was a regular figure at his local bar in Penang, drinking men half his age under the table (he did take the precaution of having the 'mama-san' bolt a stout coat hook at the appropriate height so that he could anchor the collar of his safari suit to avoid falling off his bar stool later in the evening).

What would he have made of Derby today? I think I can guess. Fred's town was one where the sight of a lone policeman was enough to disperse youngsters doing nothing more riotous than kicking a ball about. Where the arrival of a park-keeper would scatter a bunch of lads having a crafty cigarette round the back of the bowls pavilion. Where a curt shout from the conductor of a Corporation bus stifled the most innocent revelry on the top deck.

I don't need to paint the contrasting picture. We live it all the time. So, if he could come back today, Fred would certainly wonder what had gone wrong. Of course, having survived incarceration by the imperial powers of both Germany and Japan, he would soon sort out a festering (my collective noun) of shiftless feral youths.

All of which leads me, in my usual roundabout way, to tell you about an incident which, one afternoon last week, left me ever so slightly shamefaced. On a bus from Alvaston, a fight broke out between a gang of youths. Along with almost all the other passengers I was wondering whether to intervene – but leaning heavily towards letting them get on with it – when a woman in late middle age, barely five feet tall, jumped up, grabbed the biggest two and slung them off the bus with the words: 'I've been at work all day. I don't need this.'

The other recalcitrants, probably shocked that anyone – least of all that little woman – had dared intervene, also spilled on to the pavement. The rest of us? Well, I was reflecting that this might be all it takes for ordinary citizens to regain control. Of course, you'd need help from the police and the system. At the moment, even if you didn't end up a casualty, you might find yourself arrested for traumatizing a yob.

So Cousin Fred probably wouldn't think much of life in 21st-century Derby. He'd certainly wonder why smokers are forced to huddle outside pubs. Personally, I think that's the best place for them.

The Hospital That Just Grew and Grew

The courier was panting. And when he'd caught his breath, he explained that he'd had to lug the heavy parcel from the opposite side of the street, and up a bit. He couldn't park outside our house. Or even dead opposite.

Meanwhile – much more important than my delivery – an elderly neighbour had to walk unsteadily across the road to her taxi, ironically to take her to a hospital appointment.

Because we've been invaded. Invaded by what have become known around these parts as Hospital Parkers. They deserve the capital letters because they have made a capital difference to the residents of every street within reasonable walking distance of the Royal Derby Hospital.

The occasional grumpy restaurateur aside, I don't use this column for personal crusades. But everyone is suffering. Not only the locals, but also hospital staff and visitors as well, all victims of a situation that everyone – except, apparently, the people who could have done something about it – had, for years, foreseen.

Our new hospital – of which all Derbeians should be intensely proud – has grown by stealth. And now there is a price to be paid.

When the planning application was submitted in 2002, it was estimated that there would be around 4,500 staff at the hospital when it opened in 2009. The transport impact assessment and improvements to the road network for the increased traffic were agreed on that basis. The hospital was also required to prepare a plan to help manage travel to the expanded site.

Seven years on, says Councillor Lucy Care, there are almost 8,500 staff on the site, with an associated increase in patients and visitors. There is also the Nottingham University medical school, and plans to move the nursing school there. No wonder there are problems.

Why was the hospital allowed to grow apparently unchecked? Well, as a little bird in the planning department told me, it would have been politically difficult to refuse permission for subsequent extensions. It wasn't as if Tesco's wanted to add a petrol station.

Can you imagine the outcry at the headline: Council Put Block On Cancer Ward?

But now bad feeling exists between hospital and locals, which is a great pity. Good hospital facilities are surely to be welcomed?

It has been argued that shift work is a major factor because there is no adequate public transport for those coming on duty, or leaving, late at night. But the problem is largely an eight-till-five, Monday-to-Friday one. Evenings and weekends are quiet by comparison, at least in our neck of the woods. Others, of course, may tell a different story.

There is the danger of becoming a nimby here. The road outside our house isn't ours, so what right have we to complain? Well, none at all. It's just that, back in 1997, when we applied to add a bedroom to our house, before permission was granted we had to show that we could provide additional off-street parking.

Now people are allowed to park with impunity on pavements and grass verges, or so that emergency vehicles would find access difficult. So I wonder why priorities have changed.

There can't be many developments that enjoy the luxury of something like the large Kingsway Hospital site opposite Derby's new hospital. A car park big enough to accommodate everyone could have been built there. But that's another story.

In the meantime, consider this: if you applied to Derby City Council to site a business in a residential area, covering 40 acres and employing 8,500 staff, with hundreds of thousands of visitors each year, would you get away with telling the majority to park in surrounding streets? It really is a mess.

I Never Saw a Ghost in Friar Gate

I always enjoyed working in Friar Gate. Our offices were in a lovely Georgian building. There were plenty of pubs and restaurants to hand. And it was but a short, pleasant stroll into the city centre.

We were sited a few yards from the railway bridge, much-loved then, although I always used to think that, when the Great Northern Railway decided to span genteel Friar Gate, there must have been as many howls of protest from Victorian townsfolk as there would be a century later from Derbeians aghast at suggestions that the same bridge should be demolished.

There was also a family connection with that fine thoroughfare. My great-great grandfather ran the Rising Sun when it was a timber-framed inn with a thatched roof, a far cry from the pub that was rebuilt in 1888 and which today is called the Bishop Blaize.

So I had great affection for Friar Gate. Alas, commercial sense meant that, eventually, we had to move to bigger premises elsewhere. But Friar Gate remained my favourite Derby street.

Yet there was one disappointment about working there – in 15 years, I never saw a ghost.

If you believe the marketing, Friar Gate is full of ghosts. In fact, according to those who promote ghost walks, Derby is now officially the most haunted city in England. Officially? Who says so? Is there a Ministry of Ghosts and Ghouls that measures such things? If so, I'd certainly like to see the figures.

Admittedly, it's a better slogan than the one that used to run: 'Derby – The Dead Centre of England'. I wonder how long it took them to work out the irony in that.

But, as far as I was concerned, Friar Gate definitely lacked ghosts. There were plenty of creaks and groans from our ancient central heating system. But never so much as a whiff of ectoplasm. Which is surprising when you consider all the public executions that were held in the street. If you were looking for tormented souls, then a few hanged highwaymen and footpads should have provided them. Alas, none ever put in an appearance when I was locking up late on a winter's evening.

I don't discount the supernatural, any more than I would utterly refute suggestions that there might be little green men from another universe watching us right now. But this headless chain-clanking figure nonsense? Have you ever noticed that spectres promoted by the purveyors of ghost walks are almost always grey ladies, or small, sad boys, or monks, or Roman centurions? You never hear about the ghost of a Derby Corporation bus conductor, or a spooky capstan-lathe operator from Rolls-Royce. There's never a ghostly road sweeper who can't finally lay down his broom until the last piece of litter is safely in his barrow, come Judgement Day.

Actually, that may not be quite true. One website dedicated to Derby's alleged ghosts claims that, among many strange sightings reported in the Rowditch area, there is one of 'a man wearing what has been described as a donkey jacket, walking through one of the work cellars and disappearing'. Maybe that is the tortured soul of a council worker checking the drains for all eternity.

I've had a few strange sightings around there myself, although they've generally been around chucking out time, so I've always put them down to the particularly fine ale dispensed at the Rowditch Inn.

If your idea of a fun evening is having a bloke jump out from behind a tombstone with a sheet over his head, I suppose there's no harm done. It's just that, for me, Friar Gate never lived up to its reputation.

ALL QUEUING UP TO IRRITATE ME

I spent half of last Thursday in a queue. Well, in several queues, actually. Just imagine: a whole morning of your life, just shuffling along, becoming more and more irritated by other people. Which, as Mrs R will readily testify, is becoming a regular occurrence with me these days. Some of it, she says, quite irrational.

She may be right. Take this new fad that some young men have taken up, of showing their underpants above their trouser waistline. I find that irritating.

There was a gormless looking youth in the Royal Mail sorting office queue, doing just that. And it really started to annoy me. So much so that I wanted to tap him on the shoulder and say: 'Excuse me, but have you any idea how daft you look?'

Which I suppose would have been a pointless question, as he obviously didn't know. It may also have been a very unwise question because he was several inches taller than me. Which is why I didn't ask. Personally, however, when it comes to the public display of men's underpants, I'm with Eugene Williams, mayor of the Chicago suburb of Lynwood, where anyone showing three inches or more of their underwear in public is fined 25 dollars.

According to Mr Williams, young men walking around town half-dressed are keeping major retailers and economic development away. Which is something for Derby City Partnership to dwell on, perhaps?

But queuing. People have been known to join the end of a queue without knowing what was at the front of it. It happened a lot during the war. If my mother spotted a queue outside a shop, she'd join it in the hope that there'd be some onions, say, as a reward. Obviously that would only be if the queue was outside a greengrocer's. She didn't expect onions if the line had formed outside a wet fish shop (you'd be surprised at what people take the trouble to write in about, so it's as well to make the point).

Anyway, I wasn't queuing for onions at the sorting office. I was waiting to see who had sent me a letter without stamping the envelope. And it took me 20 minutes to find out because the queue reached halfway up Midland Road.

In the end, it turned out to be a newsletter that I could have done without. Especially as there wasn't just the missing 27p to pay. There was also a £1 'handling fee'. I think you should be allowed to open unstamped envelopes before deciding if you want to boost Royal Mail's profits still further. Unfortunately, the counter clerk wasn't in the mood to debate the point.

I had to join another long queue next door, in order to send a package through the post (I suppose I could have forgotten about the stamps and just bunged it in the box, but then someone at the other end would have had to queue).

Then there was the queue at the Pride Park ticket office to learn that I couldn't buy an extra two tickets for the Charlton game, at least not if I wanted the would-be spectators to actually sit together.

And, finally, there was the queue at the railway station where I discovered that the cost of a return ticket to London next week is £40.90, whereas this week, using exactly the same timed trains, it is only £29.05. Something to do with 'portions' apparently.

To be fair, the ticket clerk was very polite, even when faced with this grumpy old man. More to the point, his underpants weren't on show. Which, in my book, is always a good sign.

Why I Prefer Bakewell to Sunny Spain

It was a strange sort of lunchtime in the Mason's Arms at Mickleover. First there was the fuss because I had inadvertently trousered a tenner that didn't belong to me.

It was an innocent enough mistake, made during a chaotic five-minute spell when the egg and chip money was being collected. I'd put down my tenner, then realized I had enough change and retrieved the crisp brown note.

A few minutes later, the Travel Agent was demanding to know: 'Where's that tenner gone?' It turned out he was talking about another one that, in a senior moment, I'd also pocketed. I just forgot about the first one.

It's the honest truth, guv. But now I feel sorry for those old age pensioners who walk out of the Co-op with a tin of baked beans they've forgotten to pay for. Try telling that to the magistrate.

It has now been ruled that, when there is cash on the table, I must sit on my hands.

Anyway, the Travel Agent drained his pint and placed it down emphatically on the table in front of him, in that manner that says: 'I'm empty and it's not my round.'

Wilf, who was organizing the egg and chips, said: 'I'll get them in while I'm there.'

And when we were all replenished, Wally told this story about the Job's-worth at East Midlands Airport who almost made him miss his flight to Spain.

I should tell you that none of us have time for EMA, especially since recent alterations make it impossible to reach anywhere without first having to walk through a giant perfume shop.

Then there's selling plastic bags at two for £1 – you can't buy them singly – because the one you turned up with is the 'wrong' size for your bottles of liquid.

And I often wonder what incoming foreigners think when they

have to walk through driving rain to reach a doorway marked "International Arrivals" but that looks more like the goods entrance at Tesco's.

Back to Wally, though. He'd put his bits and bobs in one of those plastic trays and was waiting to go through the security hoop when the person in front triggered the alarm.

By the time they had been frisked, Wally had lost sight of his tray. And when he finally got to the other side, it had apparently vanished.

He was just about to raise his own alarm when Job's-worth appeared, carrying Wally's tray – actually it wasn't his tray but his belongings in another tray.

'Hey, they're mine,' said Wally.

'Well, you shouldn't have left them unattended,' said Job's-worth.

Wally was indignant: 'I didn't leave them unattended. Your lot held me up.'

'Well,' declared Job's-worth, with a definite hint of triumph in his voice, 'now you'll have to fill out this form.'

Wally thought about refusing, but there were only a few minutes remaining before the gate for his flight closed.

He was scribbling away furiously when Job's-worth spoke again.

'Now I'm going to have to take this for a liquid test,' he said, pointing to a small bottle of shower gel.

'And this will also have to be checked.' He was now holding aloft Wally's portable alarm clock.

By now Wally had steam coming out of both ears, but wiser counsel prevailed and he bit his tongue while his shower gel was tested for nitroglycerin, and his alarm clock for gelignite, and he was finally allowed to go on his way.

This is why, these days, I'm happier catching the bus to Bakewell. Plus which, if you accidentally nicked a 10 Euro note in Spain, you'd probably never see daylight again.

BANK MANAGERS – OR SMILING ASSASSINS?

Everyone else had gone out and I was sitting in the kitchen, enjoying a mug of tea with Erin and facing a dilemma when the news broke. By the way, Erin is the grey cat, a more contemplative character than her sister, Gracie. And when I say I was enjoying a mug of tea with her, obviously she wasn't drinking tea; no, she was looking out of the window, watching a sparrow hawk that, in turn, was watching a family of field mice.

And that was the dilemma: when you're preparing a meal, or washing up, you can watch these field mice scurrying about, collecting fallen bird seed. They're almost part of the family.

That's the trouble with making friends with wildlife. You get emotionally attached. Take the young wood pigeon that followed me around all last summer. This year, I'm pleased that he's got himself a girlfriend.

The question was: should I scare off the sparrow hawk? It's all part of Mother Nature's grand design. Whatever I did, the beady-eyed assassin would get his meal in the end. So I decided to let events run their natural course. Just not to tell Mrs R if one of those furry little scamps ended up as elevenses. Ignorance really is bliss.

Erin got bored and wandered off, and I went back to listening to Classic FM. I'm not high-brow (in this very column, haven't I championed the great George Formby?) but a dose of Shostakovich mid-morning never comes amiss. They should make all school kids listen to classical music. It would settle them down. Far better than that discordant dross you hear emanating from headphones. What must that do to your brain?

Anyway, it was coming up to the hour, Shostakovich gave way to a newsreader, and it was then that the story broke. The penny had finally dropped for Gordon Brown – in future banks must be run as banks, not casinos.

I've got a lot of problems with Gordon Brown, not least that when he tries to smile he looks like that character in the Batman movies. You know the one. The Joker. Pity there's nothing remotely funny about Gordon.

Pity, also, that he seems to latch on to problems about six months after the rest of the country. This business of banks getting back to basics is a prime example.

My mind went back to a morning in the HSBC Bank in St Peter's Street. There were only two counter staff to deal with two long queues of customers – not everyone wants to pay in at a machine and hope for the best – when a lass with a clipboard homed in. She was one of a number of staff patrolling the queues and she wanted to tell me that the bank had a sale on.

'Well', I said, 'if you're selling tenners for nine quid, I'll have some. But if not, wouldn't you be better employed behind a counter, helping to shorten these queues?'

Of course, it wasn't her fault. She'd been ordered to harass customers. A young journalist friend started his working life in banking, but got out because he became uncomfortable with what he was being asked to do. He'd planned to work his way up to become a kindly bank manager who helped people. Not a flash salesman peddling flash products to people who don't want them.

But kindly bank managers are a breed long consigned to memory, along with bus conductors and proper Marston's Pedigree.

Yet as I said to Erin, who'd wandered back into the kitchen, maybe now that Gordon has had his vision, Mr Mainwaring will be making a comeback.

What Happened to Gerard Street South?

Ken 'The Talker' Walker is used to the high life. Dubai, Malaysia, Sharm el Sheikh – they're on his regular schedule when he travels the globe as the world's number-one karting commentator.

Karting? I used to think it was just a load of kids bombing around in homemade soapbox trolleys. But now I know that it's the world's fastest growing motor sport, 'offering speed, thrills and great competition' if you believe my mate. Which I do. Apparently Michael Schumacher, Jensen Button and Lewis Hamilton all started off in karting. There's no need to say any more.

Ken and I grew up in the Abbey Street area, went to the same junior and grammar schools, and we've been pals for donkey's years.

A solicitor by profession, in the 1980s he got involved in Long Eaton speedway and was press officer to the British ice speedway team.

Now that he's retired from the day job, Ken works at all the top motor racing circuits, both as a track and TV commentator.

Last week, when he had a rare break before flying off to a meeting in Florida, we caught up. Not in the rarefied atmosphere of somewhere like Monaco, but rather in the down-to-earth surroundings of the Flowerpot in King Street. Well, there's a recession and I'm not on expenses.

With all this travelling, Ken is a bit out of touch with the goings-on in his home city, whereas I seem to spend most of my life wandering down memory lane. So, over a pint of a very pleasant brew called King Street Ale, I mentioned the plan to rename the Derby street where I was born and where we both went to school.

'Why's that?' asked Ken.

'Apparently it's so that the emergency services can find it, once the inner ring road is completed,' I told him.

He looked puzzled: 'Don't they already know where it is?'

'Well, you'd like to think so,' I said, 'but this is local government. There are far higher intelligences than ours at work here, old pal.'

Ken wasn't so sure. And, as it was a nice day, we supped up and went to have a look at Gerard Street, soon to become Gerard Street North.

It was purely in the interests of research, although the prospect of calling at Ye Olde Spa Inn sealed the plan.

To be honest, there wasn't much to learn. The Gerard Street of our youth is to be cut in two, but since it is all going to be called Gerard Street North – I've seen no mention of Gerard Street South – then you might as well just call it – well, Gerard Street.

It seems unfair on the people who are expected to notify, at their own expense, all sorts of organizations. So, having established that the idea was as potty in situ as it sounded in the pub, we went on our way, pausing only to look at what was once the barber's shop in Monk Street where a young Ken was despatched every week for a short-back-and-sides.

It unlatched a memory of the time his Mum sent him back because she considered that the barber hadn't taken enough off. We expected value for money in those days.

Today, the whole Abbey Street area looks sad, not least because the inner ring road is slicing through what was once a lovely community of houses and shops.

Here's a thought: maybe we could revitalize it by staging the Derby Karting Classic there, with a local lad commentating. I might mention it to whoever thought up Gerard Street North. They seem up for the occasional daft idea.

No Answer for a Nice Couple from Loughborough

They were a nice couple, crammed with the rest of us into the snug at Ye Olde Dolphin the other lunchtime. That's thing about the Dolphin: given the size of the rooms and the sort of people who frequent the pub, it's rare not to strike up a conversation with complete strangers.

The pair, from Loughborough, were in Derby to take in the city's three museums: the Wardwick, the Industrial Museum, and Pickford's House.

I found that both pleasing – and surprising. Because despite the occasional desperate efforts to talk up the place to rank somewhere alongside York or Chester, I've never really thought of Derby as a major tourist attraction.

We do have our interesting corners; and we do provide a convenient base from which to explore further afield. But as somewhere that would bring outsiders flocking in? I've never thought so.

Fortunately, the couple hadn't seen the posters for somewhere called The Lanes – 'Derby's Hidden Gems'. If they had – and expected something like Brighton's – then tramping around Babington Lane and Green Lane (don't mention the Hippodrome or Duckworth Square) would have offered up a grave disappointment. That's one promotion that should be abandoned until there's something to boast about.

It was, though, gratifying that someone had read about our museums.

I urged them to also visit the Cathedral, just a cock's stride from where we were sitting. Now there is a gem. They said they already had – and were mightily impressed.

But what they wanted to know was: what was going on at the back of the Cathedral? Who was the bloke on the horse? Why was it all being paved? And, the biggest mystery of all, why did Derby need another bridge over the Derwent, particularly one that seemed to disappear into the bowels of a block of flats?

The equestrian statue was easy to explain; the rest more difficult.

A couple of pints and a round of cheese and onion sandwiches later, I tried to work it out. Bonnie Prince Charlie looked down on a posse of skateboarders. And two middle-aged men, clutching cans of strong lager, lent on the security fence, no doubt waiting for the day when they and their ilk could take full advantage of the park benches that were tantalizingly just out of reach. Can you imagine the scene in a year's time?

And the bridge? Well it looks spectacular. And if it was on the other side of Exeter Bridge and became a feature of the Riverlights development (which we might see in about 20 years' time, when the economy has settled down and Brown's Debt has been scratched), then you might think it a decent enough project.

But try as I might, I could not come up with even the faintest of reasons why you would want a bridge connecting the back of Derby Cathedral to a block of flats. And a hugely expensive swing bridge at that.

There's a danger of sounding like those people who'd rather we still had a dirty old bus station, rows of tiny houses (by today's standards many of them unfit for human habitation) instead of Westfield, and probably Markeaton Brook still running open through the centre of town with the occasional dead dog floating past.

But for the life of me, I cannot see any possible value in the folly that is going off at the back of the Cathedral.

The project is at least a year behind schedule. It will cost ratepayers £1 million more than we were first told. And no one seems to want it anyway.

I wish I had an answer for that nice couple from Loughborough.

THE SMILING WEST INDIAN WHO LOVED CRICKET

Steve Parboo came to live near us some time in the late 1950s. Neighbours come and neighbours go, but Steve was memorable for a number of reasons, not least because he and his family were our first non-white neighbours.

Previously, the only non-white people I'd seen had been a couple of black GIs from the US Army camp at Marchington, a West Indian bus conductor in Nottingham when we went to the 1953 Test against Australia, and a door-to-door brush salesmen who wore a turban and occasionally visited houses in our street.

Steve, a West Indian of Indian descent, moved into 137 Gerard Street, a large house which had previously been run by Mrs Watkin, who took in lodgers. Lots of people seemed to have lodgers in those days; most of them single working men who often stayed with the same family for years. I suppose it was the nature of the times. Chaps coming out of the services after the war, probably well into their 30s, with no real roots anymore.

Steve also ran a guest house, in his case for fellow countrymen who arrived in Derby in increasing numbers to work in the town's factories and public service industries. Unlike the previous paying guests at 137, these chaps were in a foreign land. There must be a few old men in Derby today who, when they arrived here to start a new life, were grateful for the welcome they got from Steve.

My memory of him is a gentle man who always seemed to be wearing a smile. He was a great cricket fan, so whenever we bumped into each other, which was quite often because we lived only a few doors apart, we always had a natter.

Steve generally wanted to talk about the West Indies' 'three Ws' – Worrell, Weekes and Walcott – or that famous spin combination of Ramadhin and Valentine.

Sometimes, though, he'd let me have my head with Trueman and Statham, and my all-time favourite, Godfrey Evans. Cricket was still a lovely game in those days. So civilized.

The Parboos moved from Gerard Street in 1972 – houses in the area were scheduled for demolition – and the next time I saw him was eight years later. He was tending his front garden in Portland Street.

I can remember it as if it was yesterday – a sunny late afternoon in early August. I didn't know where the Parboos had gone after they left our neighbourhood, but there was this familiar smiling face.

We had a long chat. The West Indies were touring England that year, so this time the talk was all about Clive Lloyd and Viv Richards, Ian Botham and Geoff Boycott. Then we wished each other all the best, and that was the last time I saw him.

Years later, Steve's daughter, Garneth, got in touch. It was the 19th anniversary to the day since Steve had passed away from a heart attack at the age of 68. Her memories differed slightly from mine. Apparently Steve was a strict father.

'But, as you say, he loved cricket', said Garneth, 'and he also loved current affairs and watched every one of the news bulletins throughout the day – I'm sure you won't be surprised when I say that Sir Trevor and Moira Stewart were his favourites, although Alistair Burnett and Andrew Gardner gave them a run for their money.

'He passed away two to three weeks before Nelson Mandela was released, missed the downfall of Maggie Thatcher, the death of Diana and, obviously, Obama entering the White House.'

'How he would have loved today's 24-hour news channels.'

So he would. Here's to him . . .

Today's Footballers Don't Know They're Born

One hundred million pounds for a footballer? Half a million quid in wages every week? Now I'm convinced. The game has finally gone mad. In a week when yet another round of famous High Street names struggled to pay the rent, the fact that the Middle Eastern owners of an average Premier League club were prepared to lash out that kind of money for a player left most of the country wondering if the crazy train is now unstoppable.

It's nearly 60 years since I went to my first Derby County match at the Baseball Ground. We were playing Bolton Wanderers. My father came home from his Saturday morning stint at the *Long Eaton Advertiser* and after our fish and chips and treacle pudding and custard off we set.

It would become a familiar walk: along Gerard Street, across Burton Road and up Mount Street, then Normanton Road, Harriet Street, through the Arboretum, left into Rosehill Street, down Malcolm Street, (where householders stored bicycles for threepence for the afternoon) and into Colombo Street which led straight to the turnstiles for the Osmaston End of the Popular Side. Just to confuse me, on the way was Molineux Street: I wondered if that was where Wolves played.

Derby won 4–3. It was probably a real thriller but I can't remember. Just as, although I can say that I saw Nat Lofthouse play, to be honest, I've no recollection of him. My only clear memory of that chilly afternoon is the smell: a heady mix of Brylcreem, cigarette smoke and the stink that lingered from a week's worth of whatever they did at Ley's foundry.

It was a funny place to start a love affair. But for more than half a century, Derby County has been central to my life.

My pal John Burns – we grew up together in Gerard Street – often reminds me of the time I complained that he'd arranged his wedding to Eileen Pople for a Saturday when the Rams were due to play Rotherham United. Actually, he's wrong. It was Doncaster Rovers.

Fortunately, the formal reception ended at about half past two and, being a lot fitter in those days, I ran all the way from the Friary Hotel (12s 6d a head, by the way; it was the best place in town) and was in my usual spot on the Pop Side by kick-off. It was the only time I've watched a football match wearing a carnation buttonhole.

Football – well, life generally I suppose – was much more basic in those days. Les Moore, a centre-half built like the proverbial brick outhouse, played for Derby in the 1950s. They paid Worksop £1,000 for him and let him carry on running his insurance round.

Just by the dressing-room door at the Baseball Ground there was a jam-jar with a sticking-plaster label on which was inked: 'Les.' It was for his false teeth. As the players went out, he'd say: "OK lads, let's do it for the wife and kids."

Today's overpaid and overrated superstars might have struggled 50 years ago.

Take Ronaldo. I can never quite shake off the image of a spoiled kid pointing at a toyshop window, knowing that his mum will buy him whatever he wants.

And that pained expression when his shot goes wide. The one that says: 'That's not fair. Who moved the goalposts?'

Put him in a pair of sturdy CWS football boots, give him a football that's as heavy as a cannonball (mind the lace), stick him on the Baseball Ground mud in mid-January. Then let Les Moore tackle him.

Today's footballers? They don't know they're born.

WELL, WHAT WAS YOUR 'DIVI' NUMBER?

We were sitting in the pub when someone came up with that old chestnut: 'I bet you can remember your Co-op divi number.' And off they all went, like old soldiers trotting out their service numbers.

All except me. For some reason, my mother wasn't a member of the Co-op. I'm not sure why. We had our milk delivered by the Co-op, we took our bed linen to the Co-op laundry, and the Co-op bread van called each day. So it wasn't as if she had anything against the institution.

She was a fully paid-up member of the Awkward Squad, so maybe she just didn't like joining things. I often used to think, if Mum was in a parade of 1,000 people marching left-right, she'd be the only one going right-left.

Actually, it could be quite an endearing quality. When I was a small boy, divorced women (not divorced men, strangely enough) were ostracized. Some people didn't even like their children playing with the offspring of a divorcee.

I was allowed, though. In fact, I was actively encouraged. If she saw an underdog, a lame duck, an outsider – well, she generally wanted to stick up for them.

There was one quite refined single lady who lived round our way with her young son. I was never quite sure what she did for a living. But I did notice that she seemed to have lots of visitors. Men mostly.

When she occasionally walked up Gerard Street, on her way to the shops, there'd be adult mutterings from some of the neighbours. My mother, though, always went out of her way to greet her. Looking back, it was probably just to annoy everyone else.

If you're sharp enough, you can learn a lot from your parents. I learned to side with the outsider. And never to judge people on a first impression (Mrs R may tell you that I do have an instinctive dislike of anyone wearing a baseball hat back-to-front, but there you go).

Anyway, back to this Co-op business. Woolworth may have gone to the wall – I can't recall the last time I bought anything from Woolies – but the Co-op plough on, albeit nobody now has a divi number to remember in 50 years' time.

Derby Co-op was once a veritable empire. It seemed as if every neighbourhood had a Co-op shop. The main store, in Exchange Street, sold everything from groceries and clothing to furniture and electrical goods. The Co-op had its own building department, bakery, coal delivery business, undertakers, even a blacksmith's shop and a garage in Woods Lane to service its fleet of delivery vehicles.

People could have their houses painted and decorated by the Co-op. When we were married, the Co-op provided the cars, so I've always told people that I had a society wedding (Max Bygraves told me that one when I edited his autobiography).

In the early 1960s, the future Mrs R worked in the Co-op's ladies' corsetry department at the bottom of East Street, near the old Castle and Falcon pub.

A few years earlier, I'd been one of the many Derbeians who'd stopped to peer through a hole in the high wooden fence that surrounded the demolition of the old shops, wondering what would take its place.

Now I'd hover outside the underwear shop each evening, waiting for my girlfriend to finish work and trying not to look like some kind of pervert who was lurking about to leer at ladies' knickers.

Of course, if the constabulary had questioned me about my motives for loitering outside the Co-op, the one thing I couldn't have produced would have been my divi number.

WHICH DERBY DO YOU LIVE IN?

Back in the 1950s, comedian Terry Thomas created the character of a gap-toothed cad whose 'What an absolute shower!' became a national catchphrase.

Looking back over a year of incompetence, inefficiency, bungling and cock-ups on the part of those who govern us and care for our money, it might be time to resurrect Thomas's exasperated harangue.

Because the politicians and financiers who have messed up so spectacularly these last 12 months are just that . . . an absolute shower.

Banks lending money to people who were never likely to be able to repay it? A government whose masterstroke response was to knock tuppence-ha'penny in the pound off VAT?

You wouldn't trust any of them to run a whelk stall on Heanor market, let alone look after the interests of the nation, especially our hard-earned cash.

It's been a strange year in Derby, too. There were the theatrical farces at the Playhouse and the Hippodrome which saw the former close down and the latter all but knocked down, the plan to close most of the city's public lavatories, and the redevelopment of

Cathedral Green that ended 2008 looking like being 11 months behind schedule and costing almost a million quid more than anyone originally planned.

Oh, and we mustn't forget Quad, the £10 million Rubik's Cube lookalike that looms over the Market Place like an alien spacecraft.

Actually, I gave up attending the Playhouse years ago. I swore I wouldn't return until they fixed the air conditioning, but the quality of the productions wasn't pulling me there either.

Whichever way you slice it – and I've never bought into the theory that the building of Westfield Derby had anything to do with it – massive mismanagement is the cause of the Playhouse's ills.

The shambles at the Hippodrome should have been easier to spot. Letting someone who had applied to have the place demolished then attempt to remove a few loose slates with a giant mechanical arm was always likely to end in a cloud of brick dust.

Closing public lavatories was never likely to be a vote-winner, either. But it gives me a tenuous hook on one of my major gripes.

The Local Studies Library in Irongate has absolutely brilliant staff, but it has never boasted a public lavatory. Given that many of its users are of an age when the need to nip to the loo becomes more frequent, it's an inconvenience – just when you're halfway through a microfilm with notebooks and pencils scattered about – to be told that the nearest lavatory is in Bennett's department store (by the way, has anybody asked Bennett's if they mind?).

Either way, I can vouch that the council has never cared about ratepayers' urgent need to spend a penny.

The Cathedral Green project is more of a puzzle, not least because it has meant spending a whole load of cash on one of the city's least used areas.

The chief executive of Derby Cityscape says that it will make a major statement. Actually, it already does: that Derby is very good at wasting money on things that most of its citizens don't appear to want in the first place.

There are now two Derbys – real Derby and virtual Derby.

Virtual Derby is the one of those 'artists' impressions', the wishful thinking we'll never see because the money will never be available to build many of the pie-in-the-sky projects.

Of course, real Derby, with all its faults, is the one we live in. In the end, it's the everyday people who make it. And it's because of them that, for all I've said, I wouldn't want to live anywhere else.

Two Pianos and a Mysterious Russian

When I was a small child, our house in Gerard Street was always filled with music. My mother liked her opera, so when Enrico Caruso was scheduled for an appearance on the wireless, my father had to make do without *Variety Bandbox*.

But when the Third Programme was broadcasting something like Wagner's Ring Cycle – which seemed to go on for several days – then Dad and me could listen to the likes of the Morton Fraser Harmonica Gang on the Light Programme.

And, during holidays from Gerard Street School, I was entertained by my maternal grandmother, an excellent pianist who filled my afternoons with the popular tunes of her own, Victorian, childhood.

In fact, that upright piano she played enjoyed a place in our family folklore. During the war, my parents provided billets for soldiers from the Royal Signals who were stationed at the telephone exchange just down the road, in Colyear Street.

One of them was a Russian, some kind of electronics genius. He was also an accomplished musician who spent his off-duty hours playing classical music on that family piano, to the delight of my parents and his army colleagues alike.

Until that is, one hot summer Sunday afternoon in 1943, when two military policemen hammered on our front door, looking for the

Russian.

On that lazy afternoon, he'd been amusing himself, and entertaining the others, with a piece of Rachmaninov. Seconds later, he was leaping out of our open front-room window. He fled down Gerard Street, the red caps in pursuit, and my parents never knew his fate.

My mother, though, soon discovered that, as he'd made his escape, the mysterious Russian had grabbed a row of pearls given to her by her cousin Fred, who, before the war, had been a rubber planter in Malaya (and who, by this time, was a prisoner of the Japanese).

'Oh well,' she used to say when recounting the story (which was often), 'I suppose he was desperate.'

I still have the pre-war Russian banknote that he left behind; so perhaps there was some kind of payment for the pearls after all.

Funnily enough, my father's side also possessed a piano that became a family legend in wartime. It was a massive grand and the Rippons dived under it the night the Luftwaffe dropped bombs on the sleepy Fenland town of Spalding, hitting the Liberal club just up the road instead of their intended target, the steelworks at Peterborough, a few miles away.

So you would think that with all this music in the family – be it on the wireless, or played on famous (in my family at least) wartime pianos – that your columnist would be able to knock out a tune.

Not so. I once purchased a harmonica, complete with instruction book.

Whether it would be emulating Morton Fraser and his pals, or perhaps even Huey Lewis or Larry Adler, or simply entertaining a few friends on the porch at sundown with a mournful rendition of *Shenandoah*, I had high hopes.

Alas, the task proved beyond me, even though I didn't actually have to read music, just blow down the right numbered holes on my Hohner Great Little Harp (made in China, by the way). Two years later, I was still on the first chapter – 'Getting Started', with its sub-sections like 'Playing Single Notes' – while later chapters such as 'Making The Harp Talk', with sub-sections like 'Bending In The Up Riff', were as unreachable then as they had been when I first tore the wrapping off the instrument.

So I gave up. Since then it's been my George Formby CD and a spot of air ukulele.

A Laptop Club in Derby?

Funny isn't it – what makes people laugh? We were sitting in the pub and I was telling my companions about the new club that has opened in the old Post Office Hotel building in Victoria Street, the drinking establishment of our youth that eventually became the Spotted Horse and, subsequently, loads of other names before this current venture.

I must say that I was taken aback by their reaction: they exchanged puzzled looks, then stared at me as though I'd just announced that the ghost of George Formby had entered the Mason's Arms, ukulele in hand, and was about to give a spectral rendition of 'Mr Wu's An Air-Raid Warden Now'.

Eventually, John Cheadle, our resident travel agent, broke the silence: 'What's one of those?'

Then I realized the problem: I'd meant to say that a lap-dancing club had opened for business – I'd been past that very morning and noticed the new signage – but what I'd actually said was 'laptop club'. Slip of the tongue, of course, but it was too late to correct the mistake.

'Eh,' spluttered Paul Walton, 'I can just picture the scene: a bloke looks both ways, then sidles in, asks for a drink, and sneaks off into a dark corner, laptop under his arm, for a quick Google.'

The next five minutes descended into fits of laughter as your columnist came under merciless fire from the assembled wits.

'No, honestly,' said Cheadle in mock seriousness: 'I thought you meant it was somewhere you could have a drink while your computer was being mended.'

Still, they say that laughter is the best medicine, although, as Wally said later, you really had to be there.

Not that any of us are anticipating patronizing this addition to Derby's entertainment scene. For a start, none of us actually dare set foot in the city centre after dark.

Forty years ago, we happily strolled from the White Horse to Rick Moylan's Windmill Club, near Bass's Rec, without fear of getting into a fight.

Admittedly, we did once achieve what I suppose most people considered impossible: banishment from the Wine Vaults in the Market Place, a pub known locally as 'the Sough' which meant a drain and just about summed up the nightly goings-on there.

And come to think of it now, it was Cheadle who managed to get us barred. It must have been someone's stag night – it wasn't the sort of place we ordinarily patronized – and one of our crowd accidentally broke a glass.

The landlord demanded payment for it, but John argued that it was an accident and, in any case, he'd just handed over the money for a round for 25 people. It may have been the part where our kittymeister got to 'Now look here, my good man' that particularly annoyed mine host, but he erupted and threw us all out, for good measure banning us from ever re-entering his premises (already a highly unlikely event).

There followed the undignified sight of people furiously gulping down the ale they'd just bought before sentence was passed, but we went meekly enough; there was certainly no need to call the police. Nowadays, I'm told, on Friday and Saturday nights the constabulary park vans full of officers all around Derby's city centre, ready for violence to erupt.

I wouldn't know; by then I'm tucked up with my cocoa and the *Beano*. Nowadays, my own evening excursions are limited to the occasional midweek pint at the Rowditch Inn, which is my kind of pub: good ale, a decent crowd of regulars – and not a lap dancer in sight. Nor, come to that, even a laptop.

An Old Carpet and an Inflexible City Council

I had been holding on for the best part of half an hour, constantly being reminded that I was in a queue but that my call was important to them. So I wasn't in the best of moods when Derby City Council's refuse collection service finally got round to answering their telephone.

My request was simple enough. We'd had our front room redecorated and, in the natural order of these things, Mrs R had taken one look at the spanking new paintwork and decided that we also needed a new carpet.

Fair enough. The old one had been down since 1998, flattened by a decade of footfall, survivor of many accidents (why is it always red wine?), and I had to admit that, now, it wasn't even the right colour. I suppose I could have lived with it a bit longer. But then I'm a man and therefore not all that particular. So off to a carpet warehouse we went.

Now when you buy a new carpet, you generally have an old one of which to dispose. And this is where Derby City Council came in. Or rather didn't.

The young man who eventually picked up the phone was pleasant enough. But he had bad news: 'If it's a carpet, then that's non-domestic waste, in which case it'll cost you £30.'

That stopped me in my tracks. Quite apart from the unappealing prospect of forking out £30 just to dump a carpet, I was lost on the definition. Garages, central heating boilers, roofing, window frames, doors – I can see why they might not be acceptable; unscrupulous builders could offload a lot of their rubbish that way. But a carpet?

'Look,' I said, 'this carpet has been nailed to our front room floor for the best part of 10 years. We've watched the telly in there every evening since. I once spilled a whole pint of London Pride on it. How can it not be a domestic item?'

Of course, he was lost for an answer because he didn't make up the rules; he just followed them.

Then he had an idea: 'You could take it to the tip yourself. That would be free.'

Here we go again, I thought: the assumption that everybody on the planet owns a car.

'How would I get it on the bus?'

'Pardon?'

'I can't take it to the tip because I'm one of those eccentric beings who's never learned to drive,' I told him.

I was going to add that, if the council charges £30 just to pick up a carpet, it's small wonder that people dump rubbish down country lanes. But I suppose he would then have pointed out that, to transport a carpet to a country lane in the first place, I'd need a car. And then I could just as easily take it to the tip anyway (although that doesn't seem to stop other people littering the countryside with their cast-off freezers and bedsteads).

Feeling some affinity with those desperate people who run amok with guns in council offices, I rang off and called my mate Colin, who offered to take the carpet to the Raynesway tip for me. Obviously, I quickly added six bags of other waste (non-domestic, of course) and a broken cold frame from the garden. And all it cost me was the loan of my copy of *Eagle Annual: The Best of the 1950s Comic*.

But what if a little old lady, on a small pension, with no car owner to lean on, found herself in the same position? Would she have to fork out £30 and go without food that week? What a ridiculous rule.

A SMALL TOY AND A GOLDEN AGE OF POLITICS

I've still got the Dinky toy, tucked away in its original box. A yellow dumper truck, battered and scratched, the result of several childhood years spent playing with it in the back yard of our house in Gerard Street. It's wrapped in the original paper, too, and you can just make out the faded message, neatly written in blue ink: 'To my youngest helper with many thanks, A. Ling.'

The little toy is a relic of another age. Alderman Alec Ling was Derby's mayor in 1954. His father, Alderman Oswald Ling, had been mayor in 1922. There was once an almost dynastic approach to local politics. And that, in a roundabout way, is how I came to have that toy truck.

In October 1912, a few days after my mother was born, my maternal grandmother died from puerperal fever. My grandfather, a poorly paid horse driver at Stanton Ironworks, had three other children to support, so an aunt and uncle, who were childless, adopted the baby. From their home in Abbey Street, William Rowley ran an insurance business, his wife, Jane, a tobacconist's shop. They were much better placed to raise a new-born child.

Oswald Ling was their friend and witnessed my mother's adoption papers. So it was natural that, 40 years later, when it came to election time, my mother would want to help Oswald's son, who had himself embarked upon a life of public service.

My father didn't mind. Although his parents were Liberals who had helped to vote Henry Campbell-Bannerman into power at the 1906 General Election, Dad was 'a working-class Tory'. And the Lings were true-blue to the core. It was the only thing my parents ever agreed on. Well, that and the Beatles needing haircuts.

Anyway, it was a local election around the time of the Coronation;

Alec Ling was standing for re-election in Becket ward. I always looked forward to election day, not because I'd formed an early appreciation of the political process, but simply because I'd long since realized that wishing Becket School would burn down was a forlorn hope. At least its use as a polling station meant a rare day off.

My mother had volunteered to spend that day noting down voters' electoral numbers as they emerged. After a while, bored, I began to take the completed sheets to the party's committee room, which was situated in the front room of a tailor called Florence Clarke, opposite our house.

I made the journey scores of times until the polling station shut – that was about 9 pm in those days. Then we went to the count at the Churchill Hall in Macklin Street. Around midnight, the results were announced. Unsurprisingly in a ward where, in addition to private households, local businesses also had a vote, the incumbent Tory was returned.

Word of my efforts must have got back to Alderman Ling because, the following afternoon, he appeared with that gift, which was impressive since he must have had a hundred more important things to do in the wake of his re-election.

It's still a memory that comes back every election day – together with the question of whether the current crop of politicians measure up in any way to the likes of Alec Ling; or, in the interests of political balance, to men like Teddy Clay, the Labour chairman of the old Watch Committee, who I got to know because I went to school with his son, Stuart.

They were old-fashioned politicians, in it solely for what good they thought they might achieve, driven by principles not self-interest. They would be saddened at the way their old town is run today.

THE TROUBLE WITH PROTEST VOTING . . .

So, an election year looms. Did I ever tell you about my 12-hour political career? It was a winter's evening in 1981 when I got the call: would I put myself forward for selection as a candidate in the forthcoming Derby City Council elections? Actually, what was on offer was a hopeless task. The ward in question had been firmly in opposition hands since Adam was a lad. But it would be a sort of apprenticeship. Next time round, I'd be assured of a shoo-in.

Flattered, I agreed, was interviewed and selected. Almost immediately, though, I began to have second thoughts. A sitting councillor started moaning about the pettifogging neighbourhood disputes that took up too much of his time. To prove his point, he highlighted one particular case: a resident and her long-running argument with next-door's cat.

What had I agreed to? I wanted to help make Derby a better place. Not become pestered by spats over cats.

It was something that kept me awake all night. The following morning, I rang the party agent to resign. He was a bit cross, to be honest, because he'd just told the other hopefuls that they'd not made the cut.

'Well,' I said, 'look on the bright side. Now you can ring one of them back with some good news.'

This was in the days before spin had been recognized as an art form; and the agent wasn't convinced. But I stuck to my decision, shelving my master plan for improving Derby's lot beyond measure. Probably no one would have listened, anyway.

When I related this story to a friend, he suggested that the real weakness in local politics isn't getting bogged down with trivia; it's that the only candidates likely to succeed are, almost always, those allied to a major party. Yet local issues aren't always best served by the national policies of Conservative, Labour or Lib Dem. Sometimes, just the opposite.

He was right. But he could also have said that another flaw is that local elections are often used by voters simply to protest; therefore cities, towns and shires in our fair nation may become lumbered with ineffective councils, just because the electorate wants to kick the shins of Westminster politicians. Which is a daft reason to elect your local councillor.

Power by default can happen all too easily when one party becomes expert at harnessing the local electorate's disaffection with what is happening nationally. Months of being told how much they care, and you become the object of a one-way political love-fest.

Come the local polls, when the rest finally rouse themselves and begin popping leaflets through your letterbox, it feels right to say: 'You only hear from that lot when there's an election imminent. But these others . . . '

The trouble with protest voting is that you may wake up and find the others actually running the show. Buoyed by this, one of them might even want to become your MP; and you would have agreed to John and Edward winning *The X Factor* in exchange for that not happening.

My friend suggests that all councillors should be independent, free of national parties, standing only on local issues. It's a laudable idea, but almost a non-starter. To campaign effectively, you generally need a party machine behind you. There's a limit to how many envelopes one person can lick in a week.

For myself, even backed by an army of envelope lickers, I couldn't cope with the squabble between Mrs Bloggins and her neighbour's cat. It's never too early to mention it: whoever gets your vote, don't let them have it just to spite the other lot.

UNPLUG YOUR APPLIANCES? WHERE DO YOU START?

I was negotiating the bones in my breakfast kipper when it happened again: all our electricity went off. We'd been having trouble, for weeks. For no apparent reason, the trip switch would clunk, and everything would whirr to a standstill. The power always came straight back on again, once the switch was restored to its starting position. True, it was an inconvenience if you happened to be halfway through a televised football match. And then there was the continual resetting of alarm clocks. But we just got on with it. Now, though, disaster beckoned on a dark morning: I'd nearly choked on a smoked herring. It was time to take action.

When the electrician arrived, he did the usual tutting and brow-furrowing, and gave the sharp intakes of breath so beloved of tradesmen who like to make a mystery out of their area of expertise.

Sometimes, this is followed by 'Can't be done, me owd', before they do it anyway, just to be able to emerge a hero. That didn't seem appropriate here, although I could tell that sparks was itching to get it into his act.

Instead, he conducted some tests with what looked like a geiger-counter, announced that I had 'a fluctuation', looked very solemn, and then said: 'Right, it's obviously an appliance. Turn everything off, then switch it all back on, one by one, and we'll find out what's causing the problem.'

That's when it dawned on me why we use enough electricity in our house to power a small factory. If he'd told me the same thing 50 years ago, the task would have been simple: kettle, fire and wireless. Nowadays? Well, where do you start? We must have more appliances than Dixons.

Apart from the aforementioned, there are computers, printers, Sky box, refrigerator, freezer, washing machine (whatever happened to dolly tubs?), tumble dryer (a mangle and a clothes line used to do the trick), microwave, dishwasher, clocks, extractor fans, telephone system, garden lighting and pond pump – and that's just off the top of my head.

'Look,' I said, 'I wouldn't know where to begin. Even the TV aerial is plugged into a socket in the loft. It's going to take me days to do this. How much an hour do you charge?'

That turned out to be be irrelevant because he was on his way to another job and hadn't got days to spare anyway. So, assured that we wouldn't explode – simply be inconvenienced from time to time by a highly sensitive trip switch – I told him to leave me to it.

I'm still conducting the experiment, but it has led me to one discovery: we have a loft full of boxes for electrical appliances that we don't own any more.

It works like this: Mrs R buys a new iron, say, and the box goes into the loft, just in case the iron malfunctions during its guarantee period. But the iron works perfectly for 15 years before giving up the ghost (usually heralded by the question: 'Can you smell burning?'). We smuggle it into the dustbin, but forget about the box gathering dust in the roof space. There it lies, undisturbed, for another decade.

At the moment, we have a microwave that is awaiting disposal after someone – no names, no pack-drill – thought it a good idea to warm up something in a plastic pot. They maintain that the pot was labelled 'microwave friendly' and admittedly, as all that is left of it is now welded to the inside of the microwave, it's a claim difficult to disprove.

One thing is for certain: somewhere in our loft there'll be a box for it.

I DON'T KNOW NORMAN AND IT ISN'T HITLER'S BIRTHDAY

You come across some strange people in Post Office queues and I've always said that the trick is not to engage them in conversation. Last week, alas, I failed to follow my own advice.

I'd already made one mistake. I'd jumped off the bus at the bottom of Great Northern Road with the intention of posting my parcels at Abbey Street Post Office.

Why I hadn't remembered that the slogan 'The People's Post Office' actually means that the Government is closing them all down, and that the Abbey Street one was an early casualty, I don't know. After all, there's been enough about it in the papers.

But there I was, confronted by boarded-up windows and with no option but to walk to Victoria Street. And it was there that I met him.

He was immediately in front of me in the queue, probably in his late 60s, smelling of stale tobacco and last night's beer, a grubby polo shirt and tracksuit bottoms doing little to hide the fact that he was almost as wide as he was tall, and with a set of what I took to be home-made tattoos on his forearm (for his sake, I hope Vera is still in his life).

He grinned and said something about the length of the queue. I smiled and nodded. And then he just launched into it: 'Norman is as old as me but he was born on 2 April, and the funny thing is, Adolf Hitler was born on 1 April.'

Now I don't why I even bothered to reply, but, being a fully paid-up member of the Pedants' Union, I couldn't help myself.

'Actually,' I said, 'I think you'll find that Hitler was born on 20 April.'

It's not that I celebrate the Fuhrer's birthday, but two years ago, when I was writing a book about the 1936 Berlin Olympics, all sorts of detail stuck in my mind. That just happened to be one of them.

'No,' he said, 'it was definitely 1 April. Everyone knows that's why he was a fool. Anyway, it's all in his diaries.'

He looked around for support, but the others in the queue were all now looking either at the floor, the ceiling, or at some indeterminate point in the mid-distance and it suddenly occurred to me that they probably thought I was as daft as a brush too.

I wanted to say that the Hitler diaries were a clumsy forgery and if they hadn't actually started with 'Got up, had breakfast, invaded Poland', they might as well have. But I decided to leave it at that.

Undaunted, he changed tack: 'I've only ever stopped at one five-star hotel in my life. Never again.'

I resisted the temptation to ask what all that was about, and my new friend instead went through NHS waiting lists, the Westfield Centre (judging by the letters, he has a lot of support there) and the fact that, when he was a lot younger, he had to fight off women by the bus load.

To be honest, I wanted to return to the mysterious Norman – who, either way, doesn't share a birthday with the late leader of the Third Reich – but what fantastic journey would that have taken us on?

Fortunately, before he could tell me that he'd been in the SAS, could tell fortunes and had climbed Mount Everest, the man in the dirty shirt reached the front of the queue and was soon heading off in the direction of cashier number nine.

'What an interesting bloke,' said the man immediately behind me.

I ignored him. He could have been Norman.

A Visit to the Dentist or a Day in Court

It was a strange sort of a day. I was due to give evidence in a court case brought against the Ministry of Defence. Instead, I had a tooth out.

First, the court case: someone of my acquaintance was suing the MoD for supplying him with the wrong size boots while he was serving in Iraq.

Before I go any further, I'm sure you're asking: where does a *Derby Telegraph* columnist fit into that scenario? This weekly offering has never been filed from Basra.

Well, no, it all started in our garden. The soldier concerned, a builder by trade, was a part-time squaddie with the Territorial Army. He was called up to the Gulf War and, thanks to the British Army not always having the right equipment for our lads, spent three months in desert heat, carrying twice his own body weight of equipment on feet that clattered around in oversize footwear.

The net result was that his feet were damaged beyond repair, the MoD discharged him on medical grounds, he was suing them, and one day I just happened to ask why he was re-pointing our garden wall from a sitting position.

It turned out that it actually hurt him to stand for long and, being someone who likes to see justice done – although in my experience you should never confuse justice with the law of the land – I offered to write a letter supporting his claim that certain jobs were now beyond him.

Next thing I know, I'm being called as a witness which, to be honest, was something I was looking forward to with some relish. I fancy myself as a bit of a Rumpole of the Bailey. I bet I'd have had that MoD lawyer tied up in knots. But it wasn't to be. Two days into the case, the parties settled and my testimony wasn't needed.

Now to the tooth. When I took the call dispensing with my services as a star witness, I was just about to mount the steps of a dental surgery in yet another attempt to solve the problem of an aching tooth that the dentist had declared perfectly healthy.

This time, thank goodness, he agreed that the molar didn't deserve a clean bill of health. There were two options: root canal surgery at a cost of several hundred pounds (and it might not work) or extraction for 50 quid all in, no questions asked.

It took me all of three seconds to decide. And so on the day I should have been bamboozling the best legal brains that the Government could muster, I was instead lying back past the horizontal, staring at the ceiling and praying for a quick and merciful release.

I'm from that generation which was terrorized by the school dentist on Mill Hill Lane, so even allowing for all the advances in technique and equipment over the last 50 years, I'd still rather have been in court than in the surgery chair.

Mrs R hadn't helped. A pre-arranged shopping trip to Nottingham wasn't going to be cancelled on my behalf.

'It's only a tooth,' she said. 'A quick tug, a bit of a creak, and you'll be fine.'

'I wish you hadn't mentioned creaking,' I told her.

I needn't have worried, of course. It was all over in seconds.

The only downside was that I'd promised myself a glass or three of claret that evening, by way of aiding my recovery, but the information sheet handed to me by the dentist stated quite forcibly: no alcohol for 24 hours. Apparently it inhibits the healing process.

Rumpole of the Bailey would have been so disappointed.

It's My Palpable Peak of Lamphier

Occasionally, among those routine days when you achieve very little in between getting up and cleaning out the cat litter and going to bed with your cocoa and the *Beano*, there is a day bursting with entertainment and enlightenment.

I've just had such a day. Although, on the face of it, a visit to Ilkeston Community Hospital was an unpromising start. Incidentally, why do hospitals and schools put 'community' in their titles? Who do we think they serve? And police cars bearing slogans like: 'We fight crime.' That's reassuring; I thought they were just delivering pizza.

I have been suffering a painful, long-term, but hitherto

undiagnosed, condition in my left foot. So I was to see Tim Kilmartin, consultant podiatric surgeon. When it comes to matters *articulationes pedis*, he's the governor: veteran of 11,000 foot operations; loads of awards; lectured all over the world.

Thus, I climbed aboard Trent Barton's Black Cat service to Ilkeston and settled back. At different stops in Stanley, two elderly men – Cyril and Albert – got on. These aren't their real names but if I told you that one of them was also called Stanley, you'd get confused.

'Eye up, youth,' said Cyril. In the former Derbyshire coalfield, men well into their 80s still refer to each other as 'youth'.

'Eye up, youth,' said Albert.

'I'm going to the dentist,' volunteered Cyril. 'Two ruddy fillings.'

'Blimey, youth,' said Albert, 'you can't complain if you've still got teeth to fill at your age.'

Albert informed the entire bus that he'd had all his teeth extracted when he was 35: 'Best thing I ever did. Lack of calcium, see.'

We all nodded. Then a woman further down the bus announced that she was on her way to visit a former neighbour: 'You know that thing he had taken away? Well, it's come back.'

For a moment, I was considering weighing in with my foot, but they all seemed to know each other; a stranger trying to get in the act might have received short shrift, so I stared out of the window instead.

When I eventually presented myself to the footmeister, he gently prodded the offending joint, then asked if I did much walking.

'Quite a lot.'

'Hiking in the Derbyshire hills? Things like that?'

'Er, no,' I said, 'walking to Tesco's if I've missed the bus.'

'What about sport?' he enquired, taking a plastic skeleton of a foot from a desk drawer.

'Well,' I said, 'these days, if I feel the urge to exercise coming on,

I just lie down until it passes.'

Satisfied that he had a couch potato on his hands, Mr Kilmartin made his diagnosis: 'Palpable peak of Lamphier.'

'Come again?'

'It's also called dorsal bossing. Basically, you've got osteoarthrosis of the first metatarso-cuneiform joint.' He demonstrated on the plastic foot skeleton.

'Write it all down,' I said, 'I feel a column coming on.'

There are options: special insoles; gel pads; cortisone injections. And an operation, first described in a 1954 edition of the *Journal of Bone and Joint Surgery* (I was a *Reveille* man, myself). In those days, in a triumph of misogyny, its main aim was to get housewives back vacuuming as soon as possible.

But it involves bone grafts, metal screws, three months in plaster, and a whole year before you can kick walls again while waiting for BT to answer its helpline. Special insoles sound more appealing.

I was hoping that Cyril and Albert would also be making the return journey on the Black Cat. Then I could have said: 'Eye up, youths, my palpable peak of Lamphier isn't half playing up today.'

Top that.

Sad Story of a Millennium Tree

Every so often you learn something new. For me, last week's discovery was that Derby City Council employs people called 'tree officers'. Four of them to be precise, if the information on the UK Tree Officer Index website is up to date.

I'd never before heard of tree officers. It sounds a bit like that joke where a chap says he's found him and his mates jobs as tree fellers and one of them says: 'But there're four of us . . . '

But no, tree officers it is. Apparently most local authorities have the need for at least one arboricultural officer (as tree officers are sometime known).

Their duties usually involve managing trees in public ownership and assisting town planners in protecting suitable trees by legislation.

How did I come to find all this out? Well, it all goes back to a telephone call made to me by Mrs R the other day, not long after she'd left our house to journey into the city centre.

She'd not been gone five minutes when she called. And she sounded cross. So my first reaction was to wonder what dereliction of duty I'd been caught out on this time. My money was on the fact that, before she'd left the house, she'd probably noticed that I still hadn't broken up the pile of cardboard boxes stacked against our brown bin, a task I'd been promising to attend to as soon as the weather picked up a bit. But, no, it wasn't cardboard that had so vexed Mrs R, although it did have something to do with trees. One tree in particular, as it happened.

On the corner of Uttoxeter Road and Rough Heanor Road there had flourished a tree planted to celebrate the Millennium. Complete with commemorative plaque, it had graced that corner these past eight years.

But now, Mrs R reported, someone had chopped it down. The evidence was before her very eyes. Where recently a ten-foot tree had danced in the breeze, now only a six-inch stump bore witness to the fact that it had ever existed.

One's first thought was vandals. Or the council (which, in many people's eyes, amounts to much the same thing). Then I recalled that there had been talk of some kind of underground reservoir constructed by the corner of Rough Heanor Road; and of removing the tree to the island by the ever-mushrooming Derby City General Hospital (soon to become the Royal Derby).

But surely that would involve digging out the roots? You can't just saw down a tree, stick it in the ground, and expect it to grow. I know. I've tried it with Christmas trees and they just die on you.

It was time to consult Councillor Lucy Care, whose manifold interests included membership of the Conservation Area Advisory Committee. This probably means making sure that the Council doesn't knock down the Cathedral, but trees would probably also come under the heading of conservation.

In fact, Lucy had a full explanation for this particular tree's unfortunate demise. Apparently, moving a tree of that size was a challenge, and the tree officers were concerned that they might not be able to replace it with a reasonably sized specimen.

They found that they could buy three replacement trees of a decent size for the same cost as replanting one. Not only that, the attractive bark means that they are often planted as a group anyway, which emphasizses the trunks.

Pot-grown new trees were much more likely to settle in their new home. If the original, relocated, tree had died, it wouldn't have been replaced. See, I told you we needed tree officers.

WHEN THEY WERE CLEANING WINDOWS

It's an old joke. When we were kids, I had a part-time job as a wringer-out for a one-armed window cleaner. It's a tall story that always raises a smile from anyone who hasn't already heard it, albeit the audience is rapidly dwindling.

I assume there never really was a one-armed window cleaner. We had two excellent ones round our way: George Manning in Webster Street and Cyril Radford in Webster Street, both fine men and good neighbours whose appendages appeared to be in good working order.

I don't recall any Nelsonian polishing of the panes in 1950s inner-city Derby. With his chamois in his lone hand, how would he have held the bucket? Or, for that matter, the ladder?

But that's the funny thing about window cleaning: it's a trade that has given rise to many a comic situation because its exponents enjoy every legal reason to clamber up ladders and peer into the nation's bedrooms.

Take the late George Formby; 'When I'm Cleaning Windows' was one of his greatest hits. Then there was 1970s actor Robin Askew's film, *Confessions of a Window Cleaner*. Not that I ever saw it, you understand. Far too low-brow for a *Derby Telegraph* columnist.

Some time ago, we were entertained to a comedic interlude by a two-man window cleaning team. It was a quiet Sunday morning in Mickleover when they knocked on our door. Did we want our windows cleaning?

The answer was 'yes' because the previous chap had proved utterly useless. The likes of George Manning and Cyril Radford earned a decent living because they took pride in their work. These days, any fool with a ladder, a rag, and a bucket of dirty water thinks it an easy way to make a few bob.

Our previous window cleaner had fallen into the latter category. He'd nip up his ladder, give our windows a quick circular wipe (he didn't bother with corners), collect his seven quid, and be on to the next house before you could say: 'Oi, you've missed more than a bit!'

These two comedians nearly didn't get even that far.

'Come and look at this,' I called to Mrs R. And we watched Stan and Ollie (their real names have been changed to save them from public mockery) wrestling with their ladder. It turned out that they'd bought it only the previous day and hadn't yet worked out how to put it up.

Eventually, they managed it, one steadying it, the other wobbling up to our first floor before remembering that he hadn't taken anything with him to clean the windows.

When the job was sort of half-done, we paid them, more on the basis of entertainment value than for the fact that we now had clean windows (which, of course, we hadn't). As they tottered back to their van with the still extended ladder, I think we all knew that we wouldn't be seeing each other again.

To be fair, window cleaning can be a dangerous job. A few days before our Laurel and Hardy look-alikes, an American window cleaner had plummeted 47 storeys from a Manhattan skyscraper.

Why take the risk? Well, apparently, America is a land where window cleaners (when they aren't falling off skyscrapers) can grow rich – by £50,000 a year, according to one report.

But when it comes to champion window cleaning, look no further than home. In 2005, Britain's Terry Burrows set a world record for speedy cleaning. According to his website, Terry has carried the flag for Great Britain in window-cleaning events worldwide.

If he's coming round our way any time soon, he's got the job.

THE STRANGER WHO LOVED DERBYSHIRE

At the top of the hill, the old man paused to catch his breath. He was laden down with shopping and had probably walked up from the bus stop on the main road. It was a steep climb and we were also resting for a moment although, in our case, we were trying to hide the fact that we needed a breather by taking a special interest in the scenery across the Derwent Valley.

In fact, there was much to admire from the vantage point of Shaw Lane in Milford, which is where three old mates who grew up together in Gerard Street in post-war Derby had found themselves on their latest jaunt.

John Burns, Colin Shaw and yours truly meet up every month or so to . . . well, just wander, really. These days we have fewer constraints on our time and I often joke that our get-togethers are like *Last of the Summer Wine* without the scenery. Only on this day, we had the scenery too. And it was a backdrop that matched anything Clegg and company had ever enjoyed.

'Bit of a climb,' John said to our new companion as we all set off again.

He smiled: 'Yes, but the exercise is probably the only thing that's keeping me alive these days. And to think, I used to run up here at one time.' His accent had a faint Merseyside lilt.

'You're not from round these parts, are you?' I asked.

'Well, I have been for these last 60 years,' he said. 'I only came for a holiday, mind. I just never went back home.'

Home, it turned out, had originally been Wallasey, on the Wirral. As soon as he'd left school, early in the Second World War, he'd gone to sea. Then, when he was old enough, he'd joined the Army.

'My sister lived in Derbyshire, and my father said that she wanted me to visit her. We hadn't seen each other since 1941. I came over here and fell in love with the place straight away. I'd been in Austria for a time and it reminded me of that. Anyway, I was going for a walk one day and a chap offered me a job. So I took it and stayed. I've never regretted it. Derbyshire is the most wonderful place to live.'

Had he ever been back to Merseyside?

'Well, I went back a little while ago, and a young relative took me to look around where I grew up. I was hoping it would stir some memories but, to be honest, I didn't recognize any of it. Whoever is responsible, well they've done more damage to the place than the Luftwaffe ever did.'

Eventually, we bade him farewell and continued on our way. We wanted to see the ingeniously designed East and West Terraces on Shaw Lane, promised by the now crumpled tourist leaflet that I'd been clutching since we'd got off the bus.

'Drop in for a cup of coffee if you're coming back this way,' our new friend called after us as we parted company. Then, to underline that he was serious, he told us the number of his house.

Alas, we didn't take up his offer. Despite people making such gestures, you still feel that it would a bit of a cheek if you later pitched up on their doorstep, rattled their knocker, and said: 'Hello . . . remember us?'

But now I wish we had gone back. Chance meetings with strangers can often be so very rewarding and this one looked as if he had a lot more stories to tell. What's more, I bet he would have enjoyed telling them.

THE ONLY AIM WAS TO AVOID 'GINGER'

I don't have a regular barber. What would be the point? The time-span between visits is so vast that they would never remember me anyway. When I did try to return to the same hairdresser, in the intervening period he'd closed his shop, retired to Bournemouth, and died.

That's the problem with being follicly challenged: there is a whole side of life that now passes you by.

There was a time, of course, when I was no stranger to the barber's. 'Short back and sides and a dollop of Brylcreem, please,' was a request I regularly trotted out to Phil Vidofsky, to whose shop I was sent every fortnight in the 1950s. That was indeed a tonsorially golden time in my life.

Phil was an East End Jew of Polish descent, born in the Commercial Road. His parents moved to Derby before the First World War to live in the Little City, off Burton Road. Phil's wife, a Cohen by birth, was universally known as Bubba because she had been the baby of the family.

As I grew older, Phil became a good friend. I thought about him recently when I limped into town via Abbey Street after visiting a chiropodist (chiropodist, optician, dentist, doctor – this is why people have to retire; there's no time left to go to work).

Anyway, there I was, meandering down memory lane when I saw that the land on which Phil's shop had once stood, next to what was the Vine Inn at the bottom of Wilson Street, was still vacant.

Back in 1958, the council told Phil that they wanted his shop for the next phase of Derby's inner ring road. So off he went to work in London. He returned in 1962, to open another barber's shop in the former Thurman's tobacconist's shop at the corner of Wilson Street and Gerard Street, ironically in a direct line with where his old shop had stood, barely 100 yards away. Eventually, Phil retired. He died in 1990. It was another 20 years before they got round to building the ring road.

Not that we were without a local barber during Phil's four-year absence. There was Harry Murdock in Abbey Street, Ken Meakin in Woods Lane (for years after Ken retired, a handwritten sign – 'Service with Civility' – still gathered dust in the empty shop window) and Arthur Waplington, whose shop stood at the bottom of Grey Street, opposite the Lord Belper beer house that fell to the bulldozers in 1959.

Phil's, though, was as much a social club as a barber's shop. Bubba brought out huge steaming cups of tea to old men who gathered there every day, just to pass the time.

I'd sit there reading Tom Mix comics, occasionally looking up to watch Phil singe someone's hair with a lighted wax taper; or sharpen, on a leather belt, a fearsome looking cut-throat razor. It took me some time to work out what 'Anything for weekend, sir?' was all about.

Through the wonders of email, former Derbeian Derek Grantham, now living in Australia, told me: 'You reminded me of the regular Saturday morning trips we took as boys to the Co-op barber's shop in Albert Street. There wasn't much of a social nature there, just the fear of getting Ginger, a big RSM type who cut your hair how he liked, irrespective of what you said.

'The room had about eight barbers, each working at a mirror on the two long sides and, down the middle, a double-sided wooden seat.

You shuffled around, constantly trying to work out whom you might get. The only real aim, of course, was to avoid Ginger.'

DERBY – THE STAGE FOR THEATRICAL FARCE

If you were a cynical person, you might say that the idea of having outdoor theatre in Derby – on Cathedral Green to be precise – had been conceived solely because ours is the only major town and city in the United Kingdom not to have an indoor one. Of course, even if you were prone to cynicism on a grand scale, you'd have to ultimately admit that this wouldn't be true. Derby does have an indoor theatrical venue (it has at least three if you count the Assembly Rooms and the Guildhall) and it used to be called Derby Playhouse.

Now someone, obviously having spent a lot of time thinking about it, has come up with the alternative title of Derby Theatre. And one day – in September they say – someone, either the University of Derby or Derby City Council, will put on a show there.

Actually, if you really wanted to be creative with outdoor theatre, you could do worse than use the Hippodrome, although I suppose Health and Safety would worry, what with the place being half-demolished and all. But it is has no roof and is open to the stars, which, I should imagine, is the whole point.

But getting back to indoors, I gave up on Derby Playhouse quite some time before it went bust and, in the fall-out, everyone started accusing everyone else. I baled out well before the whole thing took on the appearance of a tragi-comedy riven by almighty egos. (Someone should write a play about it. With sweet irony it could even be put it on at Derby Theatre. Is Don Shaw about?)

Or maybe it was just an almighty cock-up. Whatever, I withdrew my patronage because the quality of productions was going down as fast as the heating was going up. If the council fix the air conditioning, I'll be back this autumn, prepared to give it another go under its new title. Not least because amateur companies will get to use the theatre, something that the previous administration should have encouraged.

The general public may never know the full story behind the demise of Derby Playhouse. It doesn't matter now. The main thing is to get the show back on the road. Or rather not in the road, but in one place.

I won't be offering my own services to the world of am-dram. I'm full of admiration for people that can learn lines and deliver them convincingly. I couldn't do it. Acting? I'd be useless at it.

I made my only stage appearance back in the 1950s, at junior school in Gerard Street, in a Christmas play written by one of the teachers who gave it the unlikely title of 'Robin Hood Meets Father Christmas' (or it could have been the other way round; anyway, they met).

I was given the part of Friar Tuck, which involved wearing a large dressing-gown stuffed with cushions, and some pink headgear edged with brown paper to give the impression of a monk's haircut (20 years later, I could have played the part without the disguise).

I've no recollection of the plot, if indeed there was one. My only memories are of speaking the lines: "There is the treasure," and then pointing dramatically to my left, only to discover that the boy deputed to bring a sack on stage had placed it to my right, contrary to everything that we had rehearsed.

I looked up and saw the red, round, jolly face of Councillor Teddy Clay, father of my pal Stuart, roaring with laughter in the depths of the audience.

I resolved there and then never to take to the stage again – indoors or out.

WHY HAVE I NEVER BEEN A TRAIN SPOTTER?

Did you know that Dvorak was a train spotter? Apparently he was a pigeon fancier too, but it was the thought of the composer hanging around Bohemian railway stations, collecting the numbers of early locos – the first steam-hauled service in his neck of the woods began in 1839, two years before he was born – that caught my imagination.

It's funny how you come across such titbits of information that send your mind wandering in all directions. In this case I was listening to Classic FM competing with the Mickleover dawn chorus – why are early birds so noisy? – and thinking about getting up, when the posh disc jockey came up with that little gem about the man who wrote the *New World Symphony*.

Just before that moment, I'd been wondering if Mrs R would remember that today was the day on which I'd promised to cut the privet hedge. She wasn't expecting topiary, you understand. No peacocks or heraldic interpretations; just the usual short back and sides (it's still a job I dislike, not least because I keep cutting through the cable).

But then this Dvorak thing came up and I put aside all thoughts of decorative hedge clipping and, instead, began to wonder why I'd never been a train spotter, especially as in the 1950s Derby offered up plenty of opportunities.

For a start, there was the Midland station as we still called it, despite the fact that the LMS Railway itself had disappeared under nationalization in 1948. Then there was Friar Gate, where we used to catch the train for day trips to Skegness. As it does today, Pear Tree and Normanton boasted a station. And there was also Nottingham Road station, near the Racecourse. Not to mention the Loco Works, where shiny new steam monsters were born in those days when Derby still boasted a huge railway industry.

So I should have been interested. Somehow, though, I never succumbed to the lure of those Ian Allen ABC books. Today, of course, you never see even a single schoolboy collecting loco numbers on Derby station. The few train spotters still lurking about station platforms today are men in late middle age, all probably pining for a 4-6-0 (bit of a defensive line-up, I always thought).

Personally, I can't recall the Age of Steam being all that pleasant. My earliest memories of train travel centre on those summers each year when we journeyed to my grandmother's home in Lincolnshire. Every time we went into a tunnel, someone had to jump out of his or her seat to pull up the carriage window, otherwise the compartment would have been filled with smoke.

It probably didn't matter. The carriages were usually so dirty that when anyone sat down, clouds of dust billowed up from the upholstery anyway. On one occasion, a previous traveller had whiled away their journey with a pencil, decorating the carriage ceiling and walls with obscene graffiti, explicit drawings and all. The train was packed and there was no opportunity to move, so everyone just sat there and tried not to look. For many, though, there was something magical about a steam train and it is an appeal that, for some, has endured.

It's not just trains, though. The other day, I was almost bowled over by a bloke running along the Morledge. He was trying to photograph one of Trent Barton's newest. Later, I overheard him discussing chassis numbers with a bus driver.

Apparently, bus spotting is a pastime in which one seeks to see all buses in a particular fleet or those produced by a particular manufacturer. No harm in that, I suppose. But you do wonder . . .

When You Knew Derby's Drunks by Name

It's a sobering thought: the amount of men – and women – breakfasting on cans of strong lager in Derby city centre. Almost everywhere the council place a bench, you can bet your bottom dollar that it won't be long before the usual sad gaggle of drunks are draped over it.

For the really serious drinking classes, Museum Square is a particular favourite; although the million quid, or whatever it was, to pave over perfectly good grass at the back of the cathedral seems to have been money well spent, at least if the intention was to provide a combined skateboard park and alcoholics' rest area.

Yet there was a time when there were so few drunks in Derby that you knew them all by name. Take James McCormick, an Irish labourer – no stereotype intended; that's what he was – who achieved local notoriety by being banned from every pub and off-licence in the town; yet still his name appeared regularly in the *Derby Telegraph* as he made yet another court appearance for being drunk and disorderly. I expect someone did his shopping for him.

McCormick's convictions ultimately surpassed three figures. He's probably a posthumous candidate for the *Guinness Book of Records*. There's irony for you.

One Saturday night, around chucking out time, I was walking past the Melbourne Arms, on Normanton Road, when a drunk was taking on half a dozen policeman trying to get him into the back of a Black Maria. Helmets littered the pavement as they struggled with him. Eventually they pinned him to the ground, one of them sitting on his chest. Suddenly, he gave an almighty roar, the bobby on his chest was catapulted into the air. And the whole battle erupted again.

I continued on my way, wondering if this was James McCormick. Alas, the *Derby Telegraph* carried no subsequent report of the incident, so I'll never know if I saw the legend in action that night.

About the only other celebrated drunks in Derby were Ronnie and Winnie Bradbury, and their companion, Lil Elliott. The trio could usually be found sitting on the windowsill of the Post Office in Victoria Street, swigging from bottles of cider. Ronnie, who'd been a seaman in his younger days, had a face sunburned almost the colour of a chestnut, and a nose flattened against his face, no doubt the result of bar-room brawls on several continents. This unholy trinity's occasional court appearances usually came after they'd caused trouble in the Labour Exchange on Normanton Road. Otherwise they never seemed to bother anyone.

Indeed, I don't remember ever feeling threatened by a drunk. Except, that is, during one Saturday lunchtime in the Bell Hotel. I was in the Dilly Bar, halfway down a pint of Bass, when a huge man with a shock of red hair strode in, snatched up my glass, drained it – and then began eating it.

There he was, biting off chunks of glass and chewing them, blood streaming from his lips. And there I was, wondering whether to congratulate him on a rarely seen party trick, or buy him another empty glass, just to be sociable. Starting an argument certainly didn't feature high on my list of options.

Fortunately, at that moment mine host wandered in from one of the other bars. His reaction was inventive: he told my new drinking chum that he was barred – for not wearing a tie. Neither was I, so I quietly slipped off my seat and disappeared into Sadler Gate without waiting for the outcome.

You could say that those days provided a young man with an unsentimental education. You certainly got a more interesting class of drunk.

What Would Pigeon Percy Make of Modern Derby?

Here's a thought. Next time you're about to tell someone that Derby isn't what it used to be, consider this: for all the design atrocities you might think have been perpetrated by more recent planners – it could have been a whole lot worse.

Imagine it. The entire city centre demolished, to be replaced by an industrial area. Almost every building from The Spot to Derby Cathedral razed to the ground to make way for a 150ft-wide road lined by seven-storey blocks. Elevated roadways along the entire length of Albert Street, over part of Victoria Street and into Green Lane, and over East Street and St Peter's Churchyard.

Horrible thought, isn't it? But, at various times in Derby's modern story, any of these might have come about.

The idea to flatten the old town centre and replace shops and houses with industrial units was floated just after the First World War.

It was a vision of how Derby might look after the Second World War that had Alderman Will Raynes telling the *Derby Evening Telegraph* in 1942: 'I would like to stand on The Spot and, looking down St Peter's Street, get a clear and unimpeded view of the beautiful tower of the Cathedral.'

And it's as recently as 1963 that Derby's councillors considered a plan to criss-cross the town centre with elevated roads and a figure-eight inner ring road. Oh, and build some high-rise council flats on The Spot.

So is it time to cut the current planners some slack? OK, probably not. But, as I said, it could have been a lot worse.

In the meantime, my mention of the perpetually drunk and disorderly James McCormick prompted Alan Hitchcock of Chaddesden to recall the day that well-known magistrates' clerk, Arthur Exton, suggested to McCormick that, considering the amount of money he had paid in fines, had he stayed reasonably sober, then the Irishman could probably have bought his own pub.

Several readers mentioned Pigeon Percy as a worthy inclusion in my pantheon of well-known local characters. Of course, Pigeon Percy – so called because he fed Derby's feral pigeons – wasn't a drunk. He just shuffled along all day, with a nub end quivering on his bottom lip.

He was almost part of the street furniture, but I never heard him speak one word. However, the late Stan Tacey, who worked at

Bemrose's printers and was, for many years, scorer to Derbyshire County Cricket Club, once told me how Percy was sitting on his own front doorstep one fine summer's day, watching workmen file back into a nearby factory after their dinner break.

'Look at that silly lot,' he told Stan, 'and they reckon I'm barmy.'

Percy would often keep Florrie Birtles company. Florrie was an *Evening Telegraph* newspaper seller whose pitch was the steps of the Boots building on the corner of St Peter's Street and East Street.

In those days, there were no little red boxes to protect sellers from the worst of Derby's weather, so Florrie was often absent, having nipped across the road to the Green Man in St Peter's Churchyard. The morose Percy was left to oversee a kind of honour system, whereby people were expected to leave the few coppers for their newspaper inside her paper-bag.

Come to think of it, Florrie was just as likely to be in the pub on a warm summer's day, so the weather probably didn't have much to do with it.

I wonder what she and Percy would make of Derby today. They'd certainly agree that it isn't what it used to be. But they might reflect that it could have been worse.

GREAT TIMES TO BE INVOLVED IN LOCAL RADIO

Derbyshire cricket supporters are upset. They say that BBC Radio Derby's coverage of their county club has dwindled almost to zero. They'd already complained that the days of ball-by-ball commentary had long gone. Now, according to some fans, even top-of-the-table matches are virtually ignored altogether.

To be honest, I wouldn't know. I've stopped listening to local radio; Classic FM for background, and the *Derby Telegraph* website for breaking local news – they now cover my daytime needs.

But if county cricket has become another casualty of BBC cuts, then we shouldn't be surprised. The corporation lost its way years ago. It has long been keener to retain the services of the foul-mouthed Jonathan Ross than it is to support decent radio. Otherwise, it would take even a fraction of Ross's £6 million annual salary and pump it into local broadcasting.

It used to be different. Back in the 1980s, I had the pleasure to work on a couple of documentary series for Radio Derby. Feedback suggested that they brought a lot of pleasure to many in the listening audience. They certainly brought me pleasure, not least because writing scripts for *Derby at War* meant working with two talented producers, Ashley Franklin and Simon Shaw.

The *Derby County Story* was even more fun. The series started out as a one-off programme, *The Day That Derby Won The Cup*, which was so well received that Bryan Harris, the recently appointed station manager, straightaway commissioned 13 programmes to mark the club's centenary. Of course, he had the budget to do it.

I regarded that particular job as a privilege. How many working days involve being paid to meet your boyhood heroes?

It was also a privilege to work with Ashley Franklin again. He was a consummate broadcaster. When the BBC let him go, it was a great loss to local radio in Derby.

Working on that Rams series gave me some amusing memories, not least of the day I struggled to keep two warring dogs apart while trying to record an interview with 1930s Welsh international, Dai Astley, at his Margate home. I managed it – just – with microphone in one hand, the other soothing a German Shepherd that was itching to pounce on the little terrier that shared its home.

There was a similar problem at the Derby home of former goalkeeper Ken Oxford. The Oxfords, a lovely couple, had a pet parrot that squawked throughout the interview. They wouldn't move it at any price. Even my jacket thrown over the cage failed to quieten it. So when I got back to the office, I threw the tape to Ashley and said: 'Best of luck.' Fortunately, his skilful editing resulted in a Polly-free interview.

Raich Carter had the kettle on when I reached his Hull home, and at Poulton-le-Fylde, Peter Doherty ushered me straight into their dining room where a table groaned with food. 'Mrs Doherty thought you might be hungry after your journey,' said the great Peter, 'so she's made you this.'

The problem was that, having arrived in the area early, I'd just treated myself to a large lunch at a Blackpool hotel. I struggled manfully through another three-course meal, recorded the interview. Then didn't eat again for about two days.

They were great times to be involved in radio. But I don't think it would now be possible for a local station to produce those sorts of series. In fact, I don't know where BBC local radio is going. Or where its target audience now lies.

I do believe that supporters of Derbyshire cricket can forget about proper match coverage. Ball-by-ball commentary won't be resumed any time soon.

DERBY'S BLACK MARKET SAW MORALS COMPROMISED

When I was growing up, down Gerard Street, in a house on the town side of Wilson Street, there lived a busy little woman who could often be seen scurrying about the neighbourhood after dusk, lugging a big sack on her back.

She'd criss-cross the street, knocking on this door and that. And if I answered her furtive tap, I'd be told, in an anxious whisper: 'Go and see if your mother wants any tea.' Almost always, my mother did want some tea – or sugar, or butter, or anything else that was in short supply – and money and consumables changed hands on our darkened front step.

114

The goods had been stolen, of course. But, in those austere days, even otherwise law-abiding housewives broke their own rules in order to put a little extra on the family table. My mother was no exception.

Because in the early post-war years, food rationing was more severe than it had been during the war. Which led to my mother making a huge compromise with her morals. Despite being scrupulously honest, almost to the point of eccentricity, there was one area where she allowed herself to dabble on the wrong side of the law: the Black Market.

Somehow, I just can't see my mother's name and the words 'receiving stolen goods' in the same sentence. But that's what it was. Albeit the circumstances were, shall we say, extenuating? At least that is what I still like to think. After all, there'd been a war on.

But if you start making excuses . . . Honesty? Where does it start? Where does it end? Is it black and white? Or will you allow shades of grey?

When I was an employer, I never minded staff making personal telephone calls, provided they first asked. When they didn't ask, and I found out, I regarded it as stealing – stealing the cost of the call, and stealing the cost of my time.

When I worked in local government, some cleaners used to nick soap and toilet rolls. They probably saw it as a perk of the job. But in my book that, too, was stealing, pure and simple.

And when I hear that someone has purchased bootleg DVDs, I regard that as dishonest because artists and production companies are deprived of their rightful royalties and profits.

Phone calls, pens, toilet rolls, sneaking out for a fag in company time, buying pirated films and music – it's a broad canvas. But where does honesty end and dishonesty begin?

Last week, I was in a Derby supermarket, transferring goods from trolley to bag, when I came across a small jar of sauce that I'd missed placing on the conveyor belt.

Eventually I found one of those self-service tills that I don't like, and persuaded a hovering member of staff to process the extra sale. But it would have been easier to wander out of the store with the sauce (it cost £1.17) claimed as some small recompense for the time, not so long ago, that the same establishment short-changed me to the tune of a tenner.

There was a long queue behind me, and I didn't want to make a fuss. So I just left my phone number and went away with the promise that they'd call me when they'd checked the till. They never did. Maybe another mistake had balanced matters.

Or perhaps their subsequent silence might have been because, when the truculent sales assistant had examined the £20 notes in her till and barked: 'Was there anything written on yours?', I'd said: 'Yes – I promise to pay the bearer.'

Honesty doesn't always pay. And neither, apparently, does sarcasm.

Taste of Austerity is Recipe for Home Cooking

It would take a twisted logic to say that economic recession is a good thing. But among the current business failures, job losses and home repossessions that make for gloomy headlines, there is one silver lining: in these cash-strapped times, more people are cooking at home. Which is good news for the nation's soul; truly, there is nothing quite like producing your own meals from fresh ingredients.

And if that's bad news for restaurateurs, well there was a time when the choice of eateries, in Derby at least, was severely limited anyway. Unlike today, when you can skip across the culinary globe in next to no time, 50 years ago it was either a hotel or a greasy spoon. There wasn't much else between the Midland Hotel's posh nosh, and beans on toast at the Old Boat Café on Cockpit Hill. Even when Berni Inns came along, there wasn't much variation. Readers with better memories than mine will remember the exact details, but for about 10 shillings (50p to the post-decimal generation) you got a very limited menu.

The future Mrs R occasionally persuaded me to take her to a Chinese restaurant that had opened above Hepworth's, the gents' outfitters, in St Peter's Street. I only ever had their mixed grill, though, which probably negated the point of visiting a Chinese in the first place. In those days, I was a callow youth, an unadventurous soul, much happier with egg and chips than egg fried rice.

But, if age brings experience, with it comes misplaced confidence. When I allowed a friend from Tokyo to order for me in a Japanese restaurant, it left a lasting impression: why anyone would want to eat raw tuna and seaweed is still quite beyond me.

And whoever encouraged the French to believe that they could cook deserves to be dunked in a vat of bouillabaisse. A survey of more than 20,000 people in 20 countries, published in the *Wall Street Journal*, saw French cuisine voted the world's most overrated. Even the French agreed.

But you have to be careful when you criticise a nation's food. Or even a county's restaurants. A few weeks ago, in this column, I ventured to suggest that the woman who'd treated us with such disdain when we'd turned up early for our table at a Derbyshire restaurant might have been in the wrong job. It was my humble opinion that people who don't like people are ill-suited for a job in a service industry. The piece prompted a string of rebukes (anonymous, of course) from someone I took to be a disaffected waiter. They certainly seemed to have a grudge against diners.

Whatever, when it comes to cuisine, haute or otherwise, only Italians should be allowed to run restaurants. They understand service, hospitality and good food better than any other nation on Earth. Some of my most memorable eating experiences have been in

Italian restaurants, not all necessarily in Italy.

Boston's North End – the Italian quarter of that great New England city – provided many of them. But my favourite had to be an Italian restaurant in Tennessee. There was good food – and atmosphere. A priest was dining in his own private booth, and every heavy, dark-suited waiter looked as if he had done serious damage to someone at sometime. It certainly wasn't the place to start an argument; a few months after we'd dined there, the restaurant was burned to the ground. I told you there was an atmosphere.

All of which is a great leap from gentle memories of the Old Boat Café. But now we mostly cook our own. Pass the recipe book.

THE HOMING PIGEON THAT WON'T GO HOME

It's been a strange week. I've been trying to catch a pigeon. Now I'm having second thoughts. It arrived one morning and sat on our back step. Initially I wasn't even sure that it was a pigeon. With a black body, white head and white wings, it looked more the result of an illicit liaison between a magpie and a dove. But it was ringed. And, as it looked young and lost, I thought I'd better try to reunite it with its owner.

There was just one thing: the last time I tried something like this, it proved a fruitless endeavour. A grey squirrel sat on our lawn for hours, looking depressed. When I rang the RSPCA, they told me to don a pair of welder's gloves – not freely available in our part of Mickleover on a Sunday afternoon – and pop it in a box. Then they would come round and kill it. Apparently you aren't allowed to give aid and succour to a grey squirrel. So I let nature take its course and the squirrel dragged itself off somewhere to die with dignity rather than by official hands.

However, homing pigeons being a whole different issue, this time I rang Alan Maris, chairman of Derby, Burton & District South Road Federation, who proved very helpful. Although if I'd thought he was going to jump in his car and come round to sort the job out himself,

Derby Hippodrome, pictured in all its pre-war grandeur. The front of the Hippodrome today, looking sad but still giving no hint of the devastation that lies behind.

The stage of the Hippodrome, pictured from Crompton Street in 2010. The damage was caused when the new owner allegedly tried to repair the roof! Until that moment it had remained largely unspoiled since the day it closed in 1959.

It could have been worse. A model of
the proposed elevated roadway through
the middle of Derby. Thank goodness
it never got further than this.

Do the years condemn? Derek Grantham,
John Cheadle, Paul Walton and Derek Taylor
pictured at Derby Bowling Alley in the 1960s,
and at the Hollybrook Tavern 40 years later.

The 1763 Assembly Rooms were damaged by fire in 1962. So Derby's council demolished them, although the facade can still be seen at the tramway museum at Crich. The new Assembly Rooms were opened in 1977. This giant television screen now dominates where the old Assembly Rooms once stood. Which do you prefer?

Exchange Street, Derby, on a winter's day in the 1980s. It obviously wasn't too dynamically stable to snow.

Derby's new bus station. Many locals mourn the passing of the Art Deco bus station on the same site, but it had become dirty and dangerous.

Duckworth Square. Was it terrorists? No, just the council.

The Quad, a £10 million arts centre that looms over Derby Market Place like an alien space craft.

Derby's tourist information centre in the brutal Assembly Rooms complex. It's enough to put off most tourists.

The bridge over the Derwent, apparently disappearing into a block of flats. It went half a million pounds over budget, and work took so long that, in the end, local taxpayers had to find almost £1 million extra.

Derby's Amen Alley, probably the only street in the city where it is possible to park illegally on both sides of the road at the same time.

More respectful days: Derby's war memorial pictured before it became the resting place for pizza–munching morons.

Stanley Guy attended Becket Junior School with me. He worked for MI5 and as an international banker before becoming an author of thrillers set in Japan. He wondered if Al-Qaeda had been busy in Derby.

Lew Patrick, pictured here pounding the streets of Derby in his late 70s.

Cousin Fred (far left, pictured with friends in Malaya) liked a smoke. He also liked a drink and hooked his jacket – he was still wearing it – to the wall of his club so that he wouldn't fall off his bar stool late into the evening.

then I was going to be disappointed. There is a homing pigeon re-homing service. But first you have to catch the bird yourself.

It turned out that our visitor was something called a black pie (don't bother to look on the internet; I've done that and all you get is recipes for pigeon pie, which certainly wasn't my intention). Anyway, Alan gave me instructions on how to go about capturing my new feathered friend. I needed two things with which I'm not blessed – patience and a quick eye – and a supply of birdseed (having first removed all the wild bird feeders so that Desmond – well I had to think a name – would become so hungry that he'd consider eating out of my hand). Oh, and if I could get him backed up against a wall, then that would be good.

When I had him, I just had to pop him in the box that I was going to use for the squirrel, read off the number on his tag, and Alan would be able to identify his owner. Simple? No.

Of course, I failed. Miserably. Every time Desmond came close and I make my move, he just flew on to the roof of the summerhouse, cocked his head on one side, and gave me a beady stare. After a few days, he disappeared altogether, so I assumed that he'd finally remembered his way home. Or perhaps our neighbourhood sparrow hawk had succeeded where I'd failed.

But now he's back. And, as in case of the sickly squirrel, it's suddenly become my view that you should let nature take its course in these matters. Especially since, unlike the squirrel, Desmond looks blissfully happy and seems to enjoy his liberty.

Incidentally, all this pigeon talk reminds me of the story of a football reporter who was covering a match at the Baseball Ground in about 1895. At half-time, he released a carrier pigeon to the *Telegraph* office, then realized that he'd forgotten to attach the score to its leg. As it flew off into the distance, the reporter cupped his hands to his mouth, and shouted after it: 'Derby County three, Small Heath nil.'

Well, it made me laugh.

GET AWAY FROM IT ALL – STAY PUT AND TAKE A PEAK

I'm not quite old enough to actually remember it, but during the Second World War there was a scheme, in Derby and elsewhere, called Holidays at Home.

The idea was to encourage beleaguered Britons to spend what little leisure time they had on their own doorsteps, rather than travel to other parts of the realm and use up resources that would have been better employed in helping defeat the funny little Austrian with the comedy moustache.

Actually, when you think about it, between 1939 and 1945 there probably wasn't much point in nipping off to Skeggy anyway. The nation's railway system was generally clogged with troops. And when you got to your seaside destination of choice, the beach would probably be covered in barbed wire and mines. So a quick paddle before high tea at Mrs Miggin's guest house was almost always going to be out of the question.

As far as I can see, irrespective of government propaganda, in those dark days the prospect of the Luftwaffe turning up to spoil a game of beach cricket meant that most folks would never have dreamt of leaving home in the first place.

Getting on for 70 years later, thanks to the recession it appears that more Britons are indeed again holidaying at home, although of course, this time 'home' means anywhere in Britain, not your actual back garden.

But are real Holidays at Home, in the wartime sense, a viable option in the 21st century? If push came to shove, could you spend an enjoyable week's vacation in Derby? Could you find enough to entertain you without ever stepping beyond the ring road?

A lot would depend on the weather. It's never much fun, for instance, wandering around Darley Park in the pouring rain. Even when the sun is blazing down from a cloudless sky, you'd struggle to spend a whole day there, once you've had a cup of tea in the café, taken a look at the National Collection of Viburnum and Hydrangea, and wondered whatever possessed the council to knock down Darley Hall.

True, for the visitor taking in Derby for the first time, there are museums and a cathedral. But I'm talking about stuff for the locals to do. Presumably most of them have already visited all the usual sights. So what else is there to keep your average Derbeian from straying far on his or her annual vacation?

Well, as much as I love the old place, I'd have to say that, to really enjoy a Holiday at Home, you would have to leave Derby and go further afield. But not that far – only into Derbyshire itself. Which, of course, is what people did in wartime. At least that's what many Derby schools did: they took parties of pupils up into the Peak District for a week of amusement, education and even edification.

So in these gloomy cash-strapped times, it might be worth considering eschewing foreign shores and plumping instead for a week of getting better acquainted with our lovely county.

Back in 1817, Lord Byron famously wrote to Thomas Moore, the man who would eventually become his literary executor: 'Was you ever in Dovedale? I can assure you there are things in Derbyshire as noble as Greece or Switzerland.' (If he was writing that today, and he'd been to Matlock Bath, he would probably add 'or Blackpool or Great Yarmouth' as a homage to Derbyshire's own seaside-resort-without-actually-having-any-sea.)

If one of Britain's greatest poets was advocating Holidays at Home back in the early 19th century, then it's good enough for me in the 21st.

What time is the next bus to Bakewell?

PUBLIC LOOS ARE THE SIGN OF A CIVILIZED SOCIETY

Personally I blame the Liberal Democrats. But, first, let us consider life's positive side. I mean, there are lots of advantages to reaching 65. A free bus pass for one. And not really caring what others think of you for another. Done it all, got the cardigan (as opposed to the T-shirt), nothing to prove – for the first time in a lifetime you can dawdle, smell the roses, visit places on your must-do list, read books you've never opened, spend long, lazy days again with friends who, like you, have been busy these last 50 years earning a living. Yes, I'm grateful for every morning that I wake up and can swing my legs out of bed.

Downsides? Well, the obvious one is that you've got a lot less time to live than you've already lived. The last 35 years have passed in a blur. I was a young man then. If I last another 35 years, I'll be expecting a congratulatory message from King William V, or whatever our dashing young prince will be called by 2044.

What has all this got to do with politics? Well, another negative to reaching pension age is that you're much more likely to have need of a public lavatory. And Derby's Lib Dem-led council wants to close a good number of our city's conveniences, replacing others with automatic flushers. That debate on the matter has been delayed does not signal victory for the protesters.

Of course, there was a time when Derby was blessed with many places in which to spend a penny, inspect the plumbing, turn your bike around, or whatever euphemism you care to use in polite company. Whenever we were in the late and lamented-only-by-some bus station, a pal of mine used to announce that he was 'going to Cheltenham', the gents' lavatory being next to the stop for the Gloucestershire spa.

In those days, I could leave the Queen's Hotel in Crompton Street on a Friday night, confident that, if nature called soon afterwards, I could take advantage of the gents' that stood by Unity Hall at the junction of Green Lane, Babington Lane and Burton Road, next to the corporation horse trough (I wonder what happened to that).

On a cold winter's morning, on my way to the Midland Station, there was the public facility in narrow Bradshaw Street, before they bulldozed the lot to make way for Bradshaw Way. Other Derbeians of a certain vintage will have their own favourites, all placed around the town to help the day run smoothly.

But now these 'branch' lavatories have all gone. And soon, if the council has its way, so too will several others, even those that I would call 'mainline' public conveniences. If they aren't removed altogether, their replacement by automatic lavatories will do little to ease the worries of an older generation. They will surely be terrified by the prospect of one day appearing in a *Derby Telegraph* headline, as they star in a real-life version of the limerick. I can see it now: 'One old lady locked in a lavatory.' Imagine the ignominy: council workers, a fire engine, a crowd of gawping onlookers. Would you want to come out?

It is my view that, along with safe streets, good health care and reliable public transport, strategically sited loos are a prerequisite for any society that wishes to describe itself as civilized. So, councillors, save the money on something else. Your travel expenses, perhaps?

One last thing: does anyone know why the hand dryers in the Westfield loos give off more decibels than a Harrier taking off from RAF Cottesmore?

STUDENTS SPURN THE BUS: ANOTHER WORRYING STATISTIC

A few years ago, I read a worrying statistic: that the number of worrying statistics had risen sharply in the previous 12 months. A worrying statistic is one that concerns the majority of the British people, and we were getting bombarded with so many statistics predicting doom and gloom that – well, we were worrying. So much so, in fact, that one MP demanded that the Government put in place stricter measures against worrying statistics.

Surprisingly, since then I've been unable to find any statistics – worrying or otherwise – to show if it did. But the fact remained that the increase in worrying statistics itself represented, you've guessed it, a worrying statistic. Which just goes to show what a load of nonsense statistics can be.

All that said, here is a worrying statistic. It appears that about 50 per cent of British children don't walk to school any more. Instead, more and more pupils are being driven there. Which means more cars than ever making needless journeys, and more kids than ever missing out on a bit of exercise and a lot of social bonding. You see it all the time in Derby.

The reasons aren't clear, although one thing is for sure: some parents are just too frightened to let their offspring out of their sight (as opposed to those parents who apparently couldn't care less that their kids are marauding the streets of our city late at night, getting all the social bonding and exercise they need as they collect their Asbos).

But whatever the cause, it is another sad development of modern life. I doubt that kids are any less safe today than they were 50 years ago. As a matter of common sense, we were told never to talk to strangers. But the possibility of us coming to harm at the hands of some weirdo wasn't at the forefront of parents' minds, as it seems to be these days. Somewhere, of course, someone will have statistics to prove, or disprove, that assertion.

Meanwhile, if the other statistics are accurate, then hundreds of thousands of children are losing out. Walking to school was one of the great delights of my childhood. You met your mates at various points before trooping off together. Those journeys were where some of my most enduring friendships were made.

They could also be an education in themselves. My Bemrose School pal, Arthur Auger, once found a dead spider in a packet of five cigarettes that he'd bought from a shop in Drewery Lane. Being good at English (but not much else), when we got to school I was enlisted to write a strong letter of complaint on Arthur's behalf. He was subsequently – and richly – compensated, although I doubt that Messrs W. D. & H. O. Wills realized that they had sent a fulsome letter of apology and 50 Woodbines to a 13-year-old schoolboy. What were the chances of that? Well, statistically . . .

The University of Derby has a statistics team that supports staff with, yes, statistics. Which brings me back to getting to lessons. The Derby students' union says that it is doing all it can to 'educate' its members to use other methods of transport, including a free shuttle bus that allows students to park and ride instead of blocking people's driveways with their cars.

Apart from wondering how allegedly cash-strapped students can afford cars in the first place, you do puzzle at how the university is going to educate them in things like strategic information technology management if they can't even be taught to catch a bus.

Maybe someone has some statistics. Then we can all start worrying.

Law and Order – Where Did It All Go Wrong?

Given the increasingly crude world in which we live, when he asked a motorist who had parked a car on the pavement – thus forcing pedestrians on to a busy road – to move it, *Derby Telegraph* reader, Dave Orford, might have anticipated a mouthful of abuse. He wouldn't have expected to be thrown down a flight of stone stairs. He certainly wouldn't have thought that, three months later, Derbyshire police would be telling him that they would be taking no action against 'the known assailant'.

Now rewind a little over half a century. It is a Saturday afternoon in November 1956. Derby County are playing away, and I am passing a loose hour by kicking a football against the wall of our house on the corner of Gerard Street and Webster Street.

Traffic wasn't a problem that day. Webster Street was a dead-end, and, anyway, no one who lived there owned a car.

On the opposite corner there stood a little grocer's shop, run by Violet Craven. I got on well with Violet, who liked a gamble. I often took her bets to an illegal turf accountant in Wilson Street. Off-course betting wasn't allowed in those days, although the police turned a collective blind eye to the bookies' offices that then proliferated in back street Derby.

What they didn't turn a blind eye to, however, was a 12-year-old boy kicking a football in the street – even if the only person likely to be really annoyed was his mother, whose afternoon of classical music was no doubt being interrupted by the steady thud of the ball rebounding off that wall.

I'd been there for about 20 minutes, wondering how the Rams were doing at Accrington Stanley, when two figures in blue turned the corner.

A few minutes later, having seen my details go into the pocket book of one Constable Robert Bromelow of Derby Borough Police – funny, I can still remember his name after all this time – I was standing crestfallen before my mother as PC Bromelow familiarized her with the by-law that I'd just transgressed. There was the possibility of a criminal charge, he said. After he had reported back to Full Street, it would be up to his superiors.

Just after the policemen had departed, leaving me quaking in my pumps, Violet's husband, Ernie, appeared. Fed up with hearing the muffled sound of my football smacking against the wall opposite, it was he who had called the police. Strangely, I never held it against him, even though he could have simply stuck his head out of his door and told me to shove off.

That teatime, my father returned from his job as a *Derby Evening Telegraph* linotype operator. On the assumption that I might yet have my collar felt, my mother thought it best to tell him of his son's brush with the law. Happily for me, he seemed more concerned with the Rams' failure to take both points at Peel Park that afternoon.

Nothing more came of it. But when I read Dave Orford's letter last week, I wondered how, in the intervening years, life had been allowed to lurch from one extreme to another. Fifty years ago, a call to the police to tell them that a small boy was kicking a football in the street was enough to bring the boys in blue running. Nowadays, you hear tales of people with burglars in the house being told that an officer might be round in a fortnight. And that throwing a man in his late 70s down a flight of stone steps doesn't even warrant a caution.

Where did it all go wrong?

No Street Lights – But We Can Enjoy the Velodrome

Another year grinds to a close. And what a strange one it has been, even by the standards of this increasingly crazy 21st century. Chief among the Alice In Wonderland feel to life in these parts recently is the fact that Derby lost out to Milton Keynes – a place that shouldn't even be allowed to have a Football League club in the first place – as a potential World Cup host city.

Yet I still resolved to end 2009 on a positive note. No chuntering – just an optimistic look ahead to next year. But then my mind kept going back to a couple of announcements made by Derby City Council as the year drew to its end.

You would have been forgiven for thinking that it was nearer All Fools' Day than New Year's Eve, when our 40-watt city council rounded off things by announcing plans to spend a large chunk of £50 million on a sporting venue of questionable value to locals, while at the same time telling us that it will be necessary to turn off the city's street lighting at night.

If I were a mugger, burglar, or just a run-of-the-mill vandal (none of whom pay council tax, I'm sure), I'd certainly think that being able to operate under cover of darkness was a lark. I wouldn't consider it such a bright idea if I was feeling my way home in the gloom and walked into a car that someone had disobligingly parked on the pavement, safe in the knowledge that the chances of a bobby catching them were about the same as mine were of being Capello's surprise call-up for the 2010 World Cup.

Then I read that the council is seriously considering spending £50 million on leisure facilities that include a velodrome-cum-concert-hall, and a swimming pool.

If it is necessary to plunge our streets into darkness in order to save taxpayers' money (and, at £3 million outlay, the jury is out on how long it would take for the scheme to pay), then forking out £50 million for the benefit of a few cyclists and swimmers seems spectacularly silly. A bit like begging a few pence for the electricity meter, then nipping out to buy a giant flat-screen telly on the never-never. Most of the money for the leisure scheme will be raised by long-term loans repayable by the taxpayer.

Paul Robinson, the city council's director of environmental services, says that it is about 'putting Derby on the map'. Last time I looked, we already were. Although, admittedly, the FA seemed to have trouble locating us in daylight, never mind in the dark.

That the council has already spent £50,000 to have consultants tell it where 1,000 times that amount might be used on the city's sporting facilities, only adds to Derbeians' despair.

A consultant is someone who borrows your watch, tells you the time, then charges you for the privilege. Example: trying to sort out its mess that has turned Littleover and parts of Mickleover into a giant parking lot, the Royal Derby Hospital employs a travel consultant; years ago, residents were queuing up to offer their own, more qualified, opinions for free. Had the NHS Trust listened, it could currently be boasting about prevention, not flailing about for cure.

Now *Derby Telegraph* readers should be consulted on ways that the city council might make better use of £50 million – road repairs, housing, care for the elderly, keeping lit the streets, that sort of thing – albeit with no great expectation that anyone at the Council House would take note.

But listen to the people. They know. In the meantime, let's all travel in hope. Happy New Year . . .

Not a Day to Feel the Christmas Spirit

He was busking: a middle-aged African Caribbean man in a Father Christmas costume, playing the ukulele – badly – and belting out a reggae version of 'Santa Claus is Coming to Town'. Who says that multi-culturalism is a bad thing? Or that Britain doesn't still have some wonderful characters? The more of both the merrier, I say.

One thing: before you start looking for this particular example of British eccentricity on your next visit to Derby's city centre, I should explain that he was spotted, not in this neck of the woods, but in Somerset, where Mrs R and I spent our annual pre-Christmas break, again pottering around the glorious city of Bath: same hotel, same pubs, same restaurants as last year; and the one before that, come to think of it.

Unadventurous? I don't care. We once spent the New Year in Singapore, which was great. But sitting in an aeroplane for 14 hours? For some years, I have officially hated airports. Europe by train from St Pancras was OK until last weekend (and if you can actually find one of those Derby to Paris fares they advertise for 50 quid return, please let me know).

In the meantime, there was a column to write and shopping to do – by now, Mrs R, who doesn't seem to mind airports, had gone to Berlin with our daughter – so, spurred on by that West Country reggae busker, I set off to investigate what Derby had to offer in street entertainment this festive season.

The answer is – not a lot; or more precisely – absolutely nothing. Not on this day, anyway. Even the bagpiper, the Eastern European violinist, and those Andean pipe players, all of whom can all be relied upon to brighten still further the sunniest summer's day, were nowhere to be seen on a bleak December morn.

Indeed, Victoria Street looked like Kettering town centre on a wet Friday, which was only half surprising since it was a wet Friday in Derby (if you think I'm being unkind to Kettering, do take a look next time you're that way).

St Peter's Street wasn't much better. Why are Derby's Christmas lights so dreary? Where were the stilt walkers, living statues, walkabout characters, magicians, puppeteers, balloon sculptors, jugglers, fire eaters, jesters, mime artists, musicians, unicyclists and face painters? I didn't get as far as Westfield. Maybe it's all going on there.

A visit to a newly opened Polish supermarket didn't raise my spirits because I couldn't read the labels. What have the Poles – lovely people, hard workers – got against vowels? Everything looks like an optician's chart.

Even the ride home disappointed. Why a woman can spend 10 minutes standing at a bus stop and realize that she has to dig deep into her shopping bag and rummage around for her purse, only when she gets on the bus, is quite beyond me.

As was the 20-something woman who broke off from arguing on a mobile phone to ask the driver what time he was leaving, and when told: 'Now,' replied: 'Can you hang on while I finish me fag?'

When he said he couldn't, she cussed before stamping out her half-smoked cigarette on the bus platform. At least she didn't waste time finding her fare. She had a free bus pass. But now I was vexed because she looked perfectly fit and I wondered how she'd qualified. It took me 60 years.

Then there was the pavement cyclist who . . . Look, I must relax. Let the world sail by. You can't beat it. Best ignore it. I'll learn to play the ukulele instead.

ECCENTRIC TEACHER TAUGHT US NOT TO TAKE LIFE SERIOUSLY

He had a shock of ginger hair, a wan complexion and a lean frame. He was bespectacled, chain-smoked, wore two pullovers (the outer one normally had a large hole) over which he pulled his underpants, and a sports coat under a flowing chalk-covered gown. He was the man who taught me never to take life – especially myself – too seriously.

It was just before Christmas when the email popped up. Richard Butt, editor of a newspaper group on the Isle of Man, was kind enough to say how much he had enjoyed an account of his grandfather that I'd included in an autobiographical memoir.

That brought memories flooding back. So I make no excuse for starting the new year with a tribute to one of Derby's greatest characters (even if he was a Yorkshireman who supported Sheffield United). Because Herbert Cook was much more than a brilliant linguist who taught modern languages at Bemrose School in the 1950s: he also imparted his enormous love of life to generations of Derby schoolboys with whom he was happy to joust verbally – provided they remembered who was ultimately in control.

He was an eccentric, was Herbert. Sometimes he'd tell a boy that he was 'enough to curdle my Weetabix'. Or he'd suddenly announce that there was 'a fortune awaiting the chap who introduces chip pans into West Germany'. A great jazz fan, one day he came into our form room, set a 78in record playing, and then just sat back and stared out of the window for the entire lesson.

There isn't room here to record all the stories about Herbert, but one from Robert Wilson, a former school captain who lived in Littleover Lane, sums him up: 'Herbert loved flights of fancy. Thus, he used the following sentence to explain to us the use of "damit" in German: "The knife with which Farrer eats his peas" – "damit" being the "with which" bit.

'One day, after this sentence had been used yet again to make the teaching point, the mild-mannered Farrer decided it was time to protest: "But I don't use a knife with which to eat peas, sir. I use a fork, like everyone else." Herbert's eyes gleamed. "Ah, Farrer," he exclaimed, "no poetry in you. No poetry." Farrer looked totally nonplussed. But that was all the answer he got.'

Herbert was a non-believer and, before he died while on holiday in the Isle of Man, insisted on nothing being said at his funeral. His grandson told me: 'Only my father, my sister, my brother and I went to Douglas crematorium because Herbert's ex-wife, Phyllis, was dying in hospital in London and their children were with her. The four of us just sat and watched the curtain close and that was that. It was probably the saddest funeral I've ever attended.'

After his death, Herbert's children spent a couple of weeks clearing his house on Uttoxeter Old Road. He'd collected so much stuff over his lifetime – records, books, manuscripts and so on – that when they got to the attic, they just left a bottle of champagne with a note that read: 'Sorry, we couldn't face it.' What a treasure trove the new owners must have found.

Would a Herbert Cook be allowed to flourish today, when 'hitting targets' seems the overriding priority? The difficulties facing modern teachers are certainly far greater than those encountered by previous generations. Where, for instance, do you start when most of your charges speak a score of different mother tongues?

Actually, that wouldn't have worried Herbert. He'd soon have learned enough of even the most obscure languages to keep everyone rolling in the aisles.

PEOPLE MIGHT MISS THE WESTFIELD CENTRE TOO

The big day dawned. Westfield Derby opened its doors, and the retail behemoth that was already resented by those Derbeians who'd rather we still had that monument to bleak 1960s Cold War architecture – the Main Centre – was up and running.

Change can indeed be a difficult prospect. We like things to stay the way they are. Sadly, it can't always be. Yes, Marks & Spencer's food hall, hitherto conveniently situated at the foot of St Peter's Street, is now halfway down London Road. But we move on.

Back in the 1870s, most Derbeians appear to have been horrified when a railway bridge was thrown across genteel Georgian Friar Gate. Patrons of the Old White Horse would have been especially peeved: the blighters knocked down their pub. But when it was suggested, some years ago, that the bridge should itself be demolished, there was a public outcry too.

I should imagine that, in the 1830s, there were townsfolk who weren't pleased when the newly formed Athenaeum Society developed land on the corner of Victoria Street and the Cornmarket, where the Royal Hotel replaced the old Red Lion and White Lion public houses.

And when, a century later, C. H. Aslin's Central Improvement plan gave us the Council House and bus station, I bet there were people who thought it would have been a better idea to leave the river bank as it was, even though it was littered with old wharves and industrial works.

As much as some people try to persuade us otherwise, Derby isn't a York or a Chester, even though we do have some magnificent architecture.

The trick is to try to integrate the old – Georgian, Victorian, Aslin's 1930s best (minus the bus station, of course) – sympathetically with the new. Do nothing and we will have neither a historic city, nor a 21st-century community; just a tired old town that hasn't changed much in 70 years.

Someone wrote to the *Derby Telegraph* claiming that Derby doesn't need city-centre hotels. Sorry, but it does. What is the alternative for St Helen's House or the former police museum in St Mary's Gate? Probable dereliction.

Derby City Council should tempt small niche retailers into areas vacated by Westfield-bound big stores. Derby could earn a reputation for having not just one of the best modern shopping centres in the country but also for offering a range of small shops where quality independent traders flourish. Like integrating old and new buildings, it's all about balance.

It's funny, though, how some folk want to cling on to the past at any price. The pre-war bus station, with its draughty, dirty, dangerous platforms, was a disgrace. How could any modern city take itself seriously when it presented that first impression to visitors?

The Riverlights? Well, anyone over the age of about 50 will recall the disused canal with its rotting barge, the cattle market and the industrial clutter, not to mention the town centre smelling of bones burning in the nearby abbatoir. The Derby Hum we used to call it.

I suppose that there are people who yearn for those days too.

Me? Well, I'm against the inner ring road blasting through the Abbey Street where I grew up. Of course, the old neighbourhood had died anyway, and mine is a reluctance based purely on nostalgia, not on any particular logic.

In 100 years time, when they want to demolish the Westfield Centre and build Derby's first space port in its stead, there'll no doubt be people writing to the *Derby Telegraph*, complaining about the demise of a much-loved shopping area that they've known for ever.

That is the problem: few of us like change.

ROLL UP! FREE LESSONS ON LIVING OFF WELFARE

Eight o'clock and it was already time to close the curtains as the nights drew in. I flipped idly through Derby City Council's latest adult learning programme. Maybe this year I'd find a course to take me through the long winter evenings, emerging into springtime with a skill I hitherto didn't know that I possessed.

I've long maintained that everyone must be world class at something, if only they could find out what skill it is that lies within them. Millions of latent talents must await discovery. I might have been a virtuoso on the Peruvian nose flute, a natural when it came to plucking the Pikasso guitar, if only I'd had the lessons.

Alas, nothing of the kind will be happening to me this year. As usual, I've found little in the council's booklet to pique my interest. The courses are top heavy on how to work computers, gain counselling skills, and understand accountancy. I already know how to get on line. I'm a dab hand at putting on the kettle and listening with a sympathetic ear, and sums not being my strong point, years ago I took the precaution of employing an accountant.

There are languages to learn, but somehow I can't be bothered. In any case, you really need to visit a country frequently to become proficient in its lingo. Many foreigners speak good English anyway. If they don't, well you can always shout at them in broken English and use rudimentary sign language. It may offend but it's always worked for me.

Wine appreciation and Italian cookery lessons beckoned briefly, but I've consumed enough wine and cooked enough Italian meals to fondly imagine that I don't need lessons in either. I hovered over Thai cooking, but I once saw this particular culinary art demonstrated by Ken Hom at the NEC, and found his subsequent book on the subject all the help I required. In fact, I went straight out and bought one of his woks.

Belly dancing, embroidery, patchwork and quilting, and furniture restoration – all definitely not me. And a 12-week course on how to use eBay seems a waste of everyone's money since it actually takes about half an hour to work it out; goodness knows how they're going to fill in two hours a week for the next three months, instructing people on how to bid for a 1954 *Beano Annual*.

I would definitely benefit from a course on health and weight management, especially the one offering keep-fit for 'mature movers', but I probably wouldn't have stuck at it.

Walking while map reading sounds too complicated; life coaching bewildering, although a recent contestant on *University Challenge* said that she was studying for a degree in something called 'enhanced motivation', which puzzled me even more.

There was one course in Derby, however, that did catch my eye: for three hours every Tuesday morning for 14 weeks at Bemrose Community School, you can find out all you need to know about claiming welfare. This will set you back £113.40, which seems a reasonable investment, given the potential returns. And if you fall into one of seven categories, one being that if you were aged between 16 and 18 on 31 August this year, then it won't cost you a bean.

Inevitably, those already on welfare won't have to pay for further education in the finer arts of living among us without actually bothering to go to work. But are we really offering school leavers free tuition in how to live off the state? That is a pretty dismal start to life in the grown-up world. Whatever happened to enhanced motivation?

MY FRIEND HAYDN: MUSIC WAS HIS LIFE

As soon as I heard the words 'according to a survey', I knew it was bad news. Sure enough, after encouraging us to drink red wine because it was good for the ticker, the medical profession is now telling us that even a modest daily glass of plonk might actually be hastening our departure from this world.

That would have disappointed an old neighbour of ours, who often invited us across the road for a glass or two of red – and then gave us a recital of classical music for good measure. He's long since passed on, but considering the instrument he played, I should think he's still in demand in that great concert hall in the sky.

It was back in the 1970s, when we lived in Overdale Road, just across the way from Haydn Atterbury, one of Britain's leading harpists. Haydn, who could read music by the time he was nine, had quite a musical pedigree. His grandfather was a harpist and violinist who had met Johann Strauss III; his father had his own string band; three uncles were all professional musicians, one of whom had played with Gustav Holst; and his granny had been principal choral soprano to Richard Wagner's personal assistant, Hans Richter.

It was Haydn's grandfather who first taught him the harp, but his big break came in 1930 when the Halle Orchestra was performing at Derby Drill Hall, among them the legendary Charles Collier, who had played the harp for Ravel and Debussy. Haydn approached the giant and asked if he would give him lessons. Over a drink in the Drill Hall Vaults, Haydn told Collier that he had saved up £30.

Collier looked him up and down and then asked: 'Would half a guinea hurt?'

Haydn later played under such legendary conductors as Sir Henry Wood, Sir Thomas Beecham and Sir Malcolm Sargent. He performed with the Halle, City of Birmingham and BBC Midlands orchestras, the English Sinfonia, and even the band of the Grenadier Guards. Locally, he was eagerly sought for after-dinner recitals and dance band work. He gave lectures at Brasenose Collage, Oxford, and played chamber music at Newstead Abbey. Once he even accompanied a mannequin parade.

All the time he lugged around his Grand Concert Morley, which stood 6ft 2ins and weighed 135lbs. Haydn told me that he bought the instrument from the Liverpool Philharmonic and tried it out for the first time in a Manchester railway waiting room on New Year's Day, 1932. That would have cheered weary travellers.

Haydn was also a fine tutor. From lessons at his home in Overdale Road, one of his pupils, Janet Evans, went to become principal harpist with the Reykjavik Symphony Orchestra. Another, John Marsden, was appointed Professor of Harp at the Royal College of Music.

By the time we arrived in Overdale Road, Haydn was still very active, but heading towards his seventies and so cutting back on his engagements. So, after dinner, we'd pop over the road, Haydn would open a bottle, produce the cigars, and give us our very own private recital while his wife, Carrie, kept the glasses filled.

He was also a wonderful raconteur. One of his favourite stories concerned the great Sir Malcolm Sargent, sitting alone on the stage after a concert pianist he was 'promoting' (Sargent was a serial womanizer) had, in rehearsal, been allowed to play something much beyond her powers.

The stage manager walked on and asked the great conductor if he wanted the piano removing.

'No,' sighed Sir Malcolm. 'Just leave it where it is . . . I'm sure it will eventually crawl off on its own.'

No Preston Plumber on *Celebrity Big Brother*

Do you ever get the feeling that life is leaving you behind? That you're trailing in its wake? I was standing at the bar of a busy hostelry in Irongate, waiting impatiently to catch the eye of the lass who seemed intent of serving everybody in the building except me, when a complete stranger asked what I thought about Vinnie Jones going into *Celebrity Big Brother*.

My initial reaction was to say: "Do I look as if I care? What is it about me that makes you think I'm the kind of person who has ever bothered to watch even one second of *Big Brother*, celebrity version or otherwise?"

But my old mum brought me up to be polite to people, even the ones asking unbelievably inane questions (actually, that's not true; she could never hide an opinion, no matter who it offended). Whatever, I just muttered something about not really having thought it through. Then carried on wondering at what point I'd become invisible to people employed to dispense beer to thirsty newspaper columnists of advancing years on Thursday lunchtimes.

Eventually, everyone else – even the stranger with the daft question – was served, and the barmaid could ignore my jumping up and down no longer. She tried her best, looking around – in some desperation, I thought – for anyone else but yours truly. But, in the end, I weaved my way back to join cousin Allan, who was by now becoming increasingly concerned about the fate of his pint of Old Maggot's Armpit (I made that up, but it was some kind of real ale) and we reflected on some of the aspects of modern culture that we have managed to bypass on life's rocky road.

It's funny, what you can safely ignore. I've never seen even one minute of *Emmerdale*. Or *East Enders*, come to that. And I gave up watching *Coronation Street* in 2001, after they killed off Alma Sedgewick, or whatever she became, by giving her cervical cancer. 'Gloom enough in real life,' I declared, reaching for the remote control to silence that familiar signature tune for the last time.

I did watch a few minutes of *Most Haunted* once. Partly because it was coming from Derby, but more in the same way that, out of morbid curiosity, you might be drawn to the scene of a bad road accident. And what about daytime television? That has to be the beginning of the end, surely?

Anyway, we finished our drinks and I looked at my watch and realized that I hadn't got time to try to get served again. Not before teatime, anyway. So we walked into the Market Place and I left Allan outside the Lock-Up Yard and went off to buy some fish, paying my respects to Steve Bloomer on the way.

Here's a name to drop: I once had a chat with Sir Tom Finney on that very spot. The Preston Plumber was at the Bloomer memorial's unveiling and recognized me from an interview I'd done with him years earlier. Imagine that – standing in the shadow of Derby Market Hall, yarning with one of the greatest footballers who ever lived. Wilf Mannion brushed past. Then Nat Lofthouse trod on my foot. I think about that every time I buy some haddock from John Eyre (who played centre-half in the old Wednesday League and trod on lots of feet).

Finney, Mannion, Lofthouse – who would have put them all together within the whiff of Derby fish market? None would have ever gone on *Celebrity Big Brother*, though. And Vinnie Jones? Well, he was never in the same class anyway.

SLIDING DOWN MEMORY LANE . . . THANKS TO AN ALARM CALL

It was embarrassing. Every few minutes, our burglar alarm went off. Which must have annoyed the neighbours no end. The alarm company were on their way, but it could be a couple of hours, they said. Inevitably, just under two hours later, the alarm stopped alarming and the engineer arrived a few minutes later.

It was 'the cold', he said. There was something called a resistor which sets things off when the temperature drops below minus 6C. We got a new alarm, this time without a resistor. The neighbours can rest in peace during subsequent cold snaps.

That said, when was the last time you saw half a dozen neighbours rush out, ready to apprehend men wearing masks and carrying sacks marked 'Swag'? You may as well leave the key in the door, 10 bottles of milk on the doorstep, and a week's worth of *Derby Telegraphs* sticking out of the letterbox.

Burglar alarms can be a nuisance. When Mrs R managed Edwards's china shop in St Peter's Street, their alarm was always going off – usually at about one in the morning. The alarm company's response was generally: 'Our engineer is in Sheffield at the moment . . .'

Anyway, our alarm sorted, and with no football on telly in snow-swept Britain, I watched an old episode of *A Place in the Sun*. A British couple were exploring houses on Vancouver Island. What a beautiful place to live. I wish that, when I was a young man, I'd had the foresight (and courage) to emigrate to Canada, just like my old mate, Bert Mozley, did years earlier.

Once, on a trip along the North-West Pacific coast, when we reached Seattle, I rang Bert (he and Jean, his wife, then lived on Galliano Island in the Gulf of Vancouver), who met us in Victoria and spent the day showing us around. Eventually, Bert pulled up outside the Empress Hotel, a grand Edwardian edifice, and said, if not exactly with a tear in his eye, then certainly with a mist forming: 'Do you know, it's 50 years to this very day since Tim and I walked up those steps for afternoon tea.' Back in 1950, Bert and his Rams team-mate, Tim Ward, had been members of the FA's Canadian tour party.

It can be an intense experience, stepping back into the footsteps of another time. Writing a book about wartime football, I painted a picture of the fateful Sunday – 3 September 1939. Central to it was the Sunderland team, including Raich Carter, the morning after their match at Highbury, gathered around a wireless set at the Russell Hotel in Russell Square, listening to Neville Chamberlain tell Britain that the nation was at war.

You'll think me daft, but last autumn, finding myself near Euston, I walked to the Russell Hotel, up the steps, through the grand doorway, into a lobby that probably hasn't changed much since the place was built, and thought, 'I'm standing on the spot where, 70 years ago today, Raich Carter heard war declared.' You could almost reach out and touch the moment.

Finally, I wish the media would simply report the weather instead of driving people's reactions to it by turning it into some kind of disaster movie. The other week, live from High Wycombe, a reporter on Sky News actually said: 'Britain is suffering a second Ice Age.' What a load of rubbish. We've had severe winters before. Just deal with it.

I mean, if I can get to the Mason's Arms of a Friday lunchtime, why can't other people get to work? I tell you, this country is going to the dogs.

Workmen Should Make the Tea

There was a polite knock on my office door and a familiar voice enquired if I would like a cup of tea. No, it wasn't Mrs R – I should be so lucky – it was the man who was decorating our front room.

'Blimey, you've got him well trained,' said my pal Colin. 'Aren't you supposed to make them tea?'

I explained: 'Well under normal circumstances, yes. But, over the years, these guys have painted and papered every nook and cranny of our house, so they're almost part of the family now.

'And the deal is that I'll provide tea, coffee, milk and sugar, but they've got to make it themselves – and include me every time.'

And, boy, was it needed at the end of a fortnight when our place had been turned upside down. Actually, it started weeks earlier, when our upstairs toilet refused to stop flushing and a plumber declared the siphon unit needed replacing. Simple enough? Not really.

The toilet is fitted into the bathroom wall, which is all very neat until you want to get the lid off the cistern. I spent the next four hours listening to all kinds of mumblings, the most recurrent of which was: 'I wish I'd never started this.' Followed by: 'I should be in a caravan at Mablethorpe by now.'

Eventually the job was done and I paid him. It was only when he was climbing into his van that he called out: 'I don't know if I've connected it properly. It's impossible to tell. Anyway, look out for water coming through your kitchen ceiling.' It wasn't the most reassuring thing I've ever been told.

But all seemed well. That is until the morning Mrs R, stopped in mid kipper and asked, as calmly as she could: 'What's that black stain over there?'

My old Bemrose School pal, David Donnelly, now owner of a property preservation company, provided the answer: 'Black spot mould, mate.'

Then he waved what looked like a TV remote control over the surface, a red light flashed alarmingly, and he delivered a damning supplementary verdict: 'Your wall is saturated.'

My instinct was to recall the plumber and demand that he put right the damage. But I couldn't face another morning of sharp intakes of breath and questions like: 'What made you buy a toilet like this in the first place?'

So instead I rang someone else, who soon uncovered the problem: the original plumber – who, to be fair, was itching to get off and start his holidays – hadn't properly sited a washer. Every time we flushed, while most of the clean water went into the cistern, some found its way into the kitchen ceiling. And after a month or two . . .

The remedy is straightforward, but first the area has to dry out. Which means that, for the last two weeks, our toilet basin has been parked on the other side of the bathroom. Fortunately we have downstairs facilities. But there's a big difference between nipping next door in the small hours, and going downstairs, waking two cats and having to explain that, no, it's not breakfast time yet; and no, I don't really want to help you play with your toy mouse.

And I've not even mentioned the blocked drain. Nor the fact that when the Council removed a lamp-post from outside our house, they nudged the fence and now our front gate hangs sadly at an unusual angle, able neither to be shut tight nor opened wide. A customer services person has taken a photograph of it and promised to get it mended.

I bet I have to make the tea, though.

SAFETY NET THAT BECAME A FEATHER BED

We had been walking around the city centre for about an hour when my old pal Stan suddenly asked the question: 'Has Derby got a particularly bad unemployment problem at the moment?'

'I don't think so,' I said. 'Why do you ask?'

'Well,' said Stan, 'I can't figure out why all these apparently able-bodied young people wandering about aren't at work. They're obviously too old to be in full-time education. Is it some kind of public holiday? I've obviously lost touch since I was last in the UK.'

'I know what you mean,' I said. 'but actually, I think for some people every day is a public holiday.'

'How come?' Stan wondered.

That started me off: 'Well you know how in any civilized country, the less fortunate are, quite rightly, provided with a safety net?'

'Of course.'

'Well, it seems that, in Britain, that safety net has become a feather bed.'

And then I jumped on to one of my hobby horses. Poor old Stan; I bet he was beginning to wish he'd never asked.

'At one time,' I said, 'it was simple: there were the haves and the have-nots. Now there are the givers – and the takers.

'The givers are the citizens who work hard all their life, paying Income Tax and National Insurance into the system. The takers are the ones who never bother to go to work, but who still enjoy a comfortable lifestyle because they're extracting what the first lot put in.'

Before we go any further, let's get one thing out of the way: I wasn't talking here about immigrants, legal or otherwise. I was talking about that certain section of the indigenous population who know every loophole in the benefits handbook.

'When you think about it,' I said, 'who is a bigger drain on society? The person, newly arrived from Romania, who spends most of his waking hours washing up in some back-street restaurant for a lot less than the minimum wage? Or the person who was born here, retired at 16 – if they lasted that long at school – and who collects a large chunk of benefits to fund their beer and fags, and probably their car and his holidays too?'

Then I told Stan a story: A friend, now just turned 60, underwent a major operation for cancer. When he was back on his feet, the medics told him that he really shouldn't work for more than 16 hours a week.

He could see the sense in that – physically and mentally he was no longer up to full-time employment – and so he accepted a modest disability allowance. It nowhere near made up the difference in his salary. But as, over 44 years, he'd paid so much into the system, he didn't feel too bad about taking something out, now that his own hour of need had arrived.

Alas, the arrangement didn't last long. My pal soon became disillusioned at the way he was grilled every time he reported in – he was made to feel like a scrounger – while the regular crowd of spongers, most of whom were on first name terms with the benefits office staff, were in and out in five minutes.

Things came to a head when the benefits office twice lost the worksheets my pal was obliged to supply. When they then denied they'd ever had them and threatened to stop his meagre payment, he'd had enough.

Upset, he told the clerk that they could keep the money. He wasn't coming back.

Her reaction? She called security and had one of the gentlest people on the planet escorted from the premises.

Sometimes, life makes you grind your teeth.

THE DAY I FELL FOUL OF THE CHAIR POLICE

I hadn't seen Ron Frost in ages. Which was odd, really, because we've been great mates for donkey's years. But circumstances change and it's not always possible to meet up as often as you'd like. So when he suggested a pint or two in the Flowerpot, just to catch up, all I said was: 'What time?'

Lots of Derbeians will know Ron. If not from the days when he was on the management team of Moorways Sport Centre, then more recently as a familiar face on the local amateur dramatics scene.

Now he spends part of his year as a holiday cowboy. In fact, a few days after we met, he was due to fly to Texas to help with the spring roundup on a working ranch. Some people really do live the dream.

We first met when Ron ran the Foresters Recreation Centre at Normanton Barracks. But it was when I joined the old Derby Borough Council as assistant manager at Derby Sports Centre (as Moorways was then known) that our friendship took off.

Looking back, I'm still not sure why I applied for the job. One quiet afternoon in April 1975, I was tearing the result of the 2.30 at Redcar off the teleprinter at the *Derby Telegraph*'s Burton office when it occurred to me that I'd been doing much the same thing in

April 1965. I suppose it just seemed time for a change.

That evening, I saw the sports centre post advertised and, before the month was out, was in the gainful employ of Derby's parks, cemeteries and allotments department. The leisure industry was a work in progress. I expect you need a degree to be a manager nowadays.

Whatever, it was the start of a roller-coaster three years, not least because the Moor Lane building had been designed by an architect who'd apparently never bothered to visit a sports centre.

But even allowing for that, it was remarkable that he'd forgotten to provide a store for the bar. Barrels of beer had to be kept in the rifle range and then rolled into the cafeteria kitchen from where the booze was siphoned up through the ceiling to the bar above.

One night, the gun club using the rifle range forgot that I was in their little ante-room, fetching a barrel of bitter, and resumed firing. It was an hour before I could re-emerge to face a couple of dozen thirsty drinkers. It did, however, enable me to continually relate the story of how I once changed a barrel of beer under gunfire.

Then there was the pettifogging bureaucracy. When someone from the management services department – time and motion, I think they used to call it – first walked into our office, his jaw dropped. When he had composed himself, he asked: 'Where did you get that chair?'

'It was here when I arrived,' I said.

'But it's got arms,' he said.

'I know,' I said.

'What grade are you on?' he asked.

When I told him, his face lit up.

'Ah,' he said, 'well in that case, you'll have to get another chair.'

It appeared that I was one grade below that which entitled me to a chair that possessed arms.

I can't tell you what I said next. After all, this is a family newspaper. But that was the point at which I decided that local government probably wasn't for me.

After a few more adventures I left and returned to newspapers. Ron stayed until he retired. So it's funny how life turns out. But then he'd probably been issued with the correct chair in the first place.

DERBY? IT'S BETTER THAN NORTHAMPTON

In 65 years, I've not moved far. Just over two miles, in fact. That's the distance between the house where I was born and the house where I now live. Why this apparent lack of an adventurous spirit? Well, I've always displayed a chronic reluctance to leave Derby, simply because the place has always suited me.

It's not too big. It's not too small. It's a convenient launching pad for getting around the UK. And the surrounding countryside isn't bad, either.

I thought about the Derbyshire countryside last week. I was spending a few days based in Northampton, travelling to various sites once connected to Britain's clandestine wartime operations – code breaking, black propaganda, secret agents, that sort of thing – partly for research, partly for amusement.

And, as we criss-crossed between Northampton and Peterborough, it struck me that, these days, the whole area is just one big retail park and distribution centre, separated only by a few sweeping new road junctions. There's no diversity and it all looks the same. I'd soon become bored if I lived in Northampton.

I said to my companion: 'Thank goodness Derbyshire is still largely unspoiled.' And I resolved to get up to Bakewell again as soon possible. The journey up the A6 never fails to delight because Derbyshire is, indeed, still a largely unspoiled county.

Which is as well, because it appears that many local people's idea of Derby is that the city itself has been spoiled quite a bit. At least that is the impression gleaned from what I've been hearing on buses and in shop queues recently.

Complete strangers fall into conversation and it's not long before one or the other comes out with the old chestnut: 'I liked Derby how it used to be.'

I suppose, in some ways, I did too. I certainly liked having a functioning theatre called the Hippodrome. And I liked the days when wandering around a few town-centre pubs of an evening was a pleasure, not my idea of what purgatory might be like.

And I liked living in Mickleover before thousands of hospital staff and tens of thousands of patients and visitors turned our street, among many others, into a free car park, complete with the contents of emptied ash trays and discarded fast-food cartons.

But, mostly, I like Derby better the way it is now. Or could be, given a little imagination on the part of the Council (considering the hospital parking fiasco, don't hold your breath), once the economic hurricane has eased.

Yesterday, I walked from one extreme to the other: from Irongate to Westfield, along the north-south spine that has defined Derby for centuries. Benjamin Franklin used to visit his mate, John Whitehurst, there, and the most famous American of his time would still recognize the ancient street today. There can't be many big towns and cities that wouldn't want an Irongate.

But there can't be many places that realistically wouldn't want a Westfield, either. The moaners claim: 'It isn't for me.' But Westfield has made London Road look better than it's ever done before in my lifetime. The new bus station complex and the Jurys Inn hotel are also beginning to give Derby the look of a serious player (forget the multi-million pound Bridge to Nowhere; that's just silly) and we might just be getting somewhere near to saying: 'Actually, it'll be nice when it's finished.'

It's just the bit in the middle that now needs sorting – Duckworth

Square and the laughably described 'hidden gems' of The Lanes (wouldn't a reopened Hippodrome have breathed new life into the area?).

No, overall, Derby is OK. Well, better than Northampton anyway.

LIFE IS ABOUT TIMING – AND HAPPY MEMORIES

The man at the bar was right: life is all about timing. I don't know what brought the subject up. But we both agreed that, to make a success of it, you generally have to be in the right place at the right time. Of course, you then have to grasp the opportunity and work it to your best advantage. But timing is everything.

Then again, you can be in the right place at the wrong time. Take the other day. The phone rang and it was a lady from the Cats' Protection League. We'd won a prize in their Christmas raffle. I rarely win anything, so my interest was piqued, even though it was unlikely to be anything more exciting than a bottle of wine. When it turned out to be a fully kitted-out make-up box, I passed the phone to Mrs R. To be fair, apparently it's a decent job, with all sorts of brushes and bits, as well as things to apply. But, as far as I was concerned, we may as well have won a set of Swahili lessons.

Anyway, back to the man at the bar. Before that, though, there is something I'd like to clear up. It seems that more than one reader has drawn the conclusion that I routinely ignore Government guidelines and spend all my waking hours on licensed premises. Not so. It's simply that pubs are a fertile ground for conversation. And when you've a column to fill . . . After all, there's a limit to how many times you can target city councillors and officials, as readily as they line up to be Aunt Sally.

So I steered my companion away from darkened street lights, cocked a deaf 'un at his desire to debate the hospital parking debacle (close to my heart though it is), ignored potholed roads and closed-down public lavatories, and instead took him down that well-worn path, good old Memory Lane. In particular, to the days when the nation's pubs were booming and when the sight of a shuttered hostelry would have been front-page news.

When I was a lad, living in Gerard Street, you could set your clock by the neighbours' drinking habits. We lived next door to a widow, Mrs Orme, and her daughter and son-in-law, Nancy and Peter Warner. Nancy was a popular figure at Boots' cosmetics counter, on the corner of East Street and St Peter's Street. Not that I was ever a patron you understand, even though, in later life, I was to win the occasional make-up box.

Peter, a shy, gentle man, worked a few minutes' walk away, as a garage mechanic in Becket Street. During the war, he'd served in the RAF, and sported a handlebar moustache to prove it, although I think he was more ground crew than fighter pilot.

On summer evenings, he and Nancy would climb into their open-top sports car, Peter wearing a cravat, Nancy all dolled up to the nines. Off they'd roar. Initially, only as far as the Durham Ox, a large white-tiled 19th-century pub that stood 200 yards away, on the corner of Gerard Street and Burton Road. In those days, however, pubs in Derby closed at 10 pm, but those in Derbyshire enjoyed an extra half-hour's drinking time. The borough boundary ended at the ring road. So, once last orders were called, Peter and Nancy didn't have far to drive. Just as far as the Half Moon on Burton Road, in fact. There, they could pull in another 30 minutes. Life, you see, has always been about timing, accidental or contrived. And about happy memories, of course.

IF YOU'RE AFTER MY VOTE – THEN SHUT THE FRONT GATE

Life is in the detail. There was a note on our doormat. Surprisingly, it was in the shape of a milk bottle (the note, not the doormat). Unsurprisingly, then, it was from someone who wanted to be our milkman.

We're keen to support local enterprise – assuming that this was local and not a dairy conglomerate masquerading as our friendly neighbourhood milkie – but I doubt we'd have taken up the offer anyway.

We stopped our milk delivery years ago. The milkman worked entirely at his own convenience. Day after day in the small hours of one scorching summer, he left milk on the doorstep to curdle (there's nothing worse than warm lumps on your Weetabix); at Christmas, he dumped 12 pints on us all in one go because he wanted a four-day holiday. I had news for him when he eventually reappeared.

But what really made me decide that this latest applicant wasn't going to get the job was in the detail: whoever had delivered the note hadn't bothered to close our front gate. If you can't shut a gate when you deliver a leaflet, it follows that you won't shut it when you make a daily milk delivery. That might not bother some people. But it bothers me. It's a lack of courtesy.

The last person before the would-be milkman not to shut our front gate was a man selling dusters. In fact, he didn't sell only dusters. He sold wind-up torches, lemon-scented antiseptic wipes, ironing board covers. And goodness knows what else.

Every time I said: 'No thanks,' he rummaged around in the bowels of a cavernous bag to produce something else that I couldn't do without. He started off politely enough, got a little tetchier with each refusal, then downright rude when he'd run out of cloths, wipes and wonder cleaners, and I still didn't want anything.

I tried reason: 'Look, I understand when you say you're trying to help yourself and not go on the dole or accept charity. But the fact is, I really don't want any of these things. So if I did buy something, then you would be accepting charity. Actually, I'm doing you a favour.' At which point, I'm sure I heard Mrs R mutter: 'You're all heart.'

Anyway, he piled everything back into his bag, swung it theatrically on to his shoulder, and flounced off, making a big point of leaving the front gate open as he went. But you know what? That bothered me less than the milkman's leaflet delivery. At least here was someone making a gesture.

I should have directed him into the city centre. He might have found a more ready market for his cleaning materials there. That is, if more fast-food outlets had pride in their businesses beyond the front door. It's about time Derby City Council forced owners to swill down the pavements outside their establishments. Get them out there every morning with a bucket of hot, soapy water and a yard brush. The only grease we want to see is elbow grease.

With elections looming, what are Derby's most important issues? There are the grandiose schemes, like velodromes, Olympic-size swimming pools, and the Riverlights. And perhaps sorting out Duckworth Square so that it looks a bit less like downtown Baghdad after a Taliban awayday. There are local issues (anyone guaranteeing to sort out the Royal Derby parking problem is a shoo-in in Littleover). And there is the detail: like cleaner pavements.

But all political parties have been warned. I won't vote for anyone who shoves a leaflet through our letterbox and then doesn't shut the front gate.

ILL FORTUNE TO WHOEVER STOLE MY SHOPPING BAG

When all is said and done, it was only a Sainsbury's carrier bag. Actually, no, it was a bit more than that. It was a Sainsbury's super shopper bag and it cost me 50p. A 'stylish, strong bag . . . designed for bulkier items and can be used and reused'. Well not by me, it can't. Not any more. Someone has nicked it.

I'll explain. It was dustbin day, as we still call it in our house. Or rather it was dustbins day, because it was the week that the council collected the blue and brown bins. And the newspapers and magazines. Which is where my Sainsbury's super shopper bag comes in. The blue plastic bag provided by Derby City Council had long given up the ghost. So we've been putting the papers in cheap plastic carrier bags. But last week, we had so many that we had to use our Sainsbury's super shopper.

Which shouldn't have caused a problem because, when they've emptied the bag, the bin men – sorry, refuse disposal operatives – always stick it in an empty bin. All you then have to do is track down where they've left the bin. It might be on next door's drive. It might be halfway down the street. The only place it won't be is where you left it. Which is irritating because, if you put it in the wrong place, then they won't collect it. So you'd like to think that they'd at least return it to the appointed spot. But they never do. And we've got used to that.

Anyway, back to my Sainsbury's super shopper bag. It was getting on for midnight when I put it out, crammed full of newspapers and magazines, leaflets offering to double-glaze us and deliver pizzas (not at the same time, obviously) and catalogues from businesses with whom we've never traded but that doesn't discourage them from bombarding us.

Then I climbed into bed, read a chapter of *Our East End* by Piers Dudgeon (good book, if you're into oral history) and floated off to sleep on the crest of my favourite dream: the one where I score the winner for Derby County against Pluto United in the Inter-Galactic Cup.

It was getting light when the cat jumped on my head. After a few minutes, I conceded defeat and went to feed her. I don't know what made me look out of the window before I opened a packet of ocean fish in gravy. But I'm glad I did. Our newspapers, magazines and junk mail were scattered halfway down Chain Lane. So, I'm now wandering up and down the street, in my dressing gown in a freezing dawn, collecting everything up. But I can't put it back in my Sainsbury's super shopper bag. Because during the early hours of a chill March night, some blackguard had emptied the contents on the pavement and made off with it.

I'm not one for retribution. But I spent the rest of the day wishing hard that some ill would befall the perpetrator. Nothing disproportionate: just a broken leg; or a severe attack of haemorrhoids; or maybe his wife running off with a refuse disposal operative (the notion of poetic justice was appealing).

I even thought of trying to invoke that Middle East curse: may your left ear wither and fall into your right pocket. But I can't see how that could happen.

When I told my pal Stuart Clay, 34 years a Derby police constable, he chuckled: 'I'm not surprised. There are people who'd pinch the milk out of your tea.'

And, it seems, Sainsbury's super shopper bags off your doorstep.

DEMOLITION DERBY LEFT US FEW ARCHITECTURAL TREASURES

So, they want to build a budget hotel next to Derby Cathedral. I wonder what Oliver Smith would say. It was over 40 years ago. I was walking through the Market Place and bumped into Oliver, then the *Derby Telegraph's* assistant circulation manager. He was quite a character. He wore a cameo brooch in the lapel of his tweed jacket, addressed you in a booming voice, and peered at you over the top of a pair of antique spectacles.

He loved his antiques, did Oliver. He also loved Derby. And on that April day in the early 1960s, we were chatting away when he suddenly looked around and said: 'You know, for all its industry, Derby still has the feel of a lovely market town.' A couple of days ago, when it was announced that Whitbread Hotels and Restaurants were interested in plonking a Premier Inn in the heart of the Cathedral Quarter, I thought about that moment. And panicked.

Oliver was right. It was probably Derby's best era. Not that we should have stood still in the years that followed. But, oh, how our city could have been modernized without destroying so many of its architectural gems. And without building so many hideous replacements.

It's astonishing, what has disappeared since the war. The Old Mayor's Parlour in Tenant Street, one of England's largest Tudor urban residences, demolished for no apparent reason. Darley and Markeaton Halls, destroyed after being allowed to fall into neglect. The 16th-century Nottingham Castle Inn in St Michael's Lane, needlessly pulled down.

When the 18th-century Assembly Rooms were damaged by fire, they were demolished; another town might have found another way. When St Alkmund's and its Georgian churchyard made way for the inner ring road, we wondered: was there really no alternative?

Other cities rebuilt their railway stations and still managed to retain handsome 19th-century facades. Not Derby. When the council took its eye off the wrecking ball, a large chunk of the Hippodrome came crashing down.

How ironic that Derby's attempts to become a tourist attraction come only after the wholesale loss of buildings that would have been a huge asset to such an initiative.

It's not all bad, of course. Irongate is still a joy, especially around the Cathedral – at the moment. Looking west, with the Guildhall on your left, the Market Place still presents an attractive face (except when obscured by a marquee full of Lady Boys from Bangkok). But turn around. The 1970s Assembly Rooms wouldn't have looked out of place in Soviet Russia. And if there are places that the Quad might suit, Derby Market Place doesn't happen to be one of them.

Elsewhere in the city centre, the exterior of what is now Derby Theatre looks like a fire station. And if the old Castle and Falcon wouldn't have won any awards for architectural excellence, whoever approved its replacement must have been an admirer of the bunkers in Hitler's Atlantic Wall.

That end of East Street is a mess. The most positive thing about the empty Riverlights complex is that it doesn't look out of place set against the Eagle Market across the road.

When you weigh up what Derby's planners have allowed over the last half century, there aren't too many that you'd have let design you a garden shed, never mind a city centre. Maybe they just weren't paying attention when the artists' impressions were dropped on the table. Maybe it was always late on a Friday and they were hurrying to go home. Let's hope that this time they find a moment to have a good look at the drawings. There's precious little left to save.

IF YOU'RE AFTER MY VOTE – THEN SHUT THE FRONT GATE

Life is in the detail. There was a note on our doormat. Surprisingly, it was in the shape of a milk bottle (the note, not the doormat). Unsurprisingly, then, it was from someone who wanted to be our milkman.

We're keen to support local enterprise – assuming that this was local and not a dairy conglomerate masquerading as our friendly neighbourhood milkie – but I doubt we'd have taken up the offer anyway.

We stopped our milk delivery years ago. The milkman worked entirely at his own convenience. Day after day in the small hours of one scorching summer, he left milk on the doorstep to curdle (there's nothing worse than warm lumps on your Weetabix); at Christmas, he dumped 12 pints on us all in one go because he wanted a four-day holiday. I had news for him when he eventually reappeared.

But what really made me decide that this latest applicant wasn't going to get the job was in the detail: whoever had delivered the note hadn't bothered to close our front gate. If you can't shut a gate when you deliver a leaflet, it follows that you won't shut it when you make a daily milk delivery. That might not bother some people. But it bothers me. It's a lack of courtesy.

The last person before the would-be milkman not to shut our front gate was a man selling dusters. In fact, he didn't sell only dusters. He sold wind-up torches, lemon-scented antiseptic wipes, ironing board covers. And goodness knows what else.

Every time I said: 'No thanks,' he rummaged around in the bowels of a cavernous bag to produce something else that I couldn't do without. He started off politely enough, got a little tetchier with each refusal, then downright rude when he'd run out of cloths, wipes and wonder cleaners, and I still didn't want anything.

I tried reason: 'Look, I understand when you say you're trying to help yourself and not go on the dole or accept charity. But the fact is, I really don't want any of these things. So if I did buy something, then you would be accepting charity. Actually, I'm doing you a favour.' At which point, I'm sure I heard Mrs R mutter: 'You're all heart.'

Anyway, he piled everything back into his bag, swung it theatrically on to his shoulder, and flounced off, making a big point of leaving the front gate open as he went. But you know what? That bothered me less than the milkman's leaflet deliver. At least here was someone making a gesture.

I should have directed him into the city centre. He might have found a more ready market for his cleaning materials there. That is, if more fast-food outlets had pride in their businesses beyond the front door. It's about time Derby City Council forced owners to swill down the pavements outside their establishments. Get them out there every morning with a bucket of hot, soapy water and a yard brush. The only grease we want to see is elbow grease.

With elections looming, what are Derby's most important issues? There are the grandiose schemes, like velodromes, Olympic-size swimming pools, and the Riverlights. And perhaps sorting out Duckworth Square so that it looks a bit less like downtown Baghdad after a Taliban awayday. There are local issues (anyone guaranteeing to sort out the Royal Derby parking problem is a shoo-in in Littleover). And there is the detail: like cleaner pavements.

But all political parties have been warned. I won't vote for anyone who shoves a leaflet through our letterbox and then doesn't shut the front gate.

Ill Fortune to Whoever Stole My Shopping Bag

When all is said and done, it was only a Sainsbury's carrier bag. Actually, no, it was a bit more than that. It was a Sainsbury's super shopper bag and it cost me 50p. A 'stylish, strong bag . . . designed for bulkier items and can be used and reused'. Well not by me, it can't. Not any more. Someone has nicked it

I'll explain. It was dustbin day, as we still call it in our house. Or rather it was dustbins day, because it was the week that the council collected the blue and brown bins. And the newspapers and magazines. Which is where my Sainsbury's super shopper bag comes in. The blue plastic bag provided by Derby City Council had long given up the ghost. So we've been putting the papers in cheap plastic carrier bags. But last week, we had so many that we had to use our Sainsbury's super shopper.

Which shouldn't have caused a problem because, when they've emptied the bag, the bin man – sorry, refuse disposal operative – always sticks it in an empty bin. All you then have to do is track down where they've left the bin. It might be on next door's drive. It might be halfway down the street. The only place it won't be is where you left it. Which is irritating because, if you put it in the wrong place, then they won't collect it. So you'd like to think that they'd at least return it to the appointed spot. But they never do. And we've got used to that.

Anyway, back to my Sainsbury's super shopper bag. It was getting on for midnight when I put it out, crammed full of newspapers and magazines, leaflets offering to double-glaze us and deliver pizzas (not at the same time, obviously) and catalogues from businesses with whom we've never traded but that doesn't discourage them from bombarding us.

Then I climbed into bed, read a chapter of <I>Our East End<I> by Piers Dudgeon (good book, if you're into oral history) and floated off to sleep on the crest of my favourite dream: the one where I score the winner for Derby County against Pluto United in the Inter-Galactic Cup.

It was getting light when the cat jumped on my head. After a few minutes, I conceded defeat and went to feed her. I don't know what made me look out of the window before I opened a packet of ocean fish in gravy. But I'm glad I did. Our newspapers, magazines and junk mail were scattered halfway down Chain Lane. So, I'm now wandering up and down the street, in my dressing gown in a freezing dawn, collecting everything up. But I can't put it back in my Sainsbury's super shopper bag. Because during the early hours of a chill March night, some blackguard had emptied the contents on the pavement and made off with it.

I'm not one for retribution. But I spent the rest of the day wishing hard that some ill would befall the perpetrator. Nothing disproportionate: just a broken leg; or a severe attack of haemorrhoids; or maybe his wife running off with a refuse disposal operative (the notion of poetic justice was appealing).

I even thought of trying to invoke that Middle East curse: may your left ear wither and fall into your right pocket. But I can't see how that could happen.

When I told my pal Stuart Clay, 34 years a Derby police constable, he chuckled: 'I'm not surprised. There are people who'd pinch the milk out of your tea.'

And, it seems, Sainsbury's super shopper bags off your doorstep.

DEMOLITION DERBY LEFT US FEW ARCHITECTURAL TREASURES

So, they want to build a budget hotel next to Derby Cathedral. I wonder what Oliver Smith would say. It was over 40 years ago. I was walking through the Market Place and bumped into Oliver, then the *Derby Telegraph*'s assistant circulation manager. He was quite a character. He wore a cameo brooch in the lapel of his tweed jacket, addressed you in a booming voice, and peered at you over the top of a pair of antique spectacles.

He loved his antiques, did Oliver. He also loved Derby. And on that April day in the early 1960s, we were chatting away when he suddenly looked around and said: 'You know, for all its industry, Derby still has the feel of a lovely market town.' A couple of days ago, when it was announced that Whitbread Hotels and Restaurants were interested in plonking a Premier Inn in the heart of the Cathedral Quarter, I thought about that moment. And panicked.

Oliver was right. It was probably Derby's best era. Not that we should have stood still in the years that followed. But, oh, how our city could have been modernized without destroying so many of its architectural gems. And without building so many hideous replacements.

It's astonishing, what has disappeared since the war. The Old Mayor's Parlour in Tenant Street, one of England's largest Tudor urban residences, demolished for no apparent reason. Darley and Markeaton Halls, destroyed after being allowed to fall into neglect. The 16th-century Nottingham Castle Inn in St Michael's Lane, needlessly pulled down.

When the 18th-century Assembly Rooms were damaged by fire, they were demolished; another town might have found another way. When St Alkmund's and its Georgian churchyard made way for the inner ring road, we wondered: was there really no alternative?

Other cities rebuilt their railway stations and still managed to retain handsome 19th-century facades. Not Derby. When the council took its eye off the wrecking ball, a large chunk of the Hippodrome came crashing down.

How ironic that Derby's attempts to become a tourist attraction come only after the wholesale loss of buildings that would have been a huge asset to such an initiative.

It's not all bad, of course. Irongate is still a joy, especially around the Cathedral – at the moment. Looking west, with the Guildhall on your left, the Market Place still presents an attractive face (except when obscured by a marquee full of Lady Boys from Bangkok). But turn around. The 1970s Assembly Rooms wouldn't have looked out of place in Soviet Russia. And if there are places that the Quad might suit, Derby Market Place doesn't happen to be one of them.

Elsewhere in the city centre, the exterior of what is now Derby Theatre looks like a fire station. And if the old Castle and Falcon wouldn't have won any awards for architectural excellence, whoever approved its replacement must have been an admirer of the bunkers in Hitler's Atlantic Wall.

That end of East Street is a mess. The most positive thing about the empty Riverlights complex is that it doesn't look out of place set against the Eagle Market across the road.

When you weigh up what Derby's planners have allowed over the last half century, there aren't too many that you'd have let design you a garden shed, never mind a city centre. Maybe they just weren't paying attention when the artists' impressions were dropped on the table. Maybe it was always late on a Friday and they were hurrying to go home. Let's hope that this time they find a moment to have a good look at the drawings. There's precious little left to save.